To my beloved friend Elinor –

    With enormous gratitude
for the gift of sitting by
her stream and listening
to the gentle flow of her
great heart.

              Bonheur, toujours,
            Marguerite

STREAMS
of
CONTENTMENT

STREAMS
of
CONTENTMENT

Lessons I Learned on My Uncle's Farm

ROBERT J. WICKS

Author of *Riding the Dragon*

SORIN BOOKS Notre Dame, Indiana

Related Books by Robert J. Wicks

Bounce: Living the Resilient Life (Oxford, 2010)

Riding the Dragon: 10 Lessons for Inner Strength in Challenging Times (Sorin Books, 2003)

© 2011 by Robert J. Wicks

www.avemariapress.com

ISBN-10 1-933495-27-8 ISBN-13 978-1-933495-27-9

Cover image © Thinkstock.

Cover and text design by Brian C. Conley.

Printed and bound in the United States of America.

Library of Congress Cataloging-in-Publication Data

Wicks, Robert J.
  Streams of contentment : lessons I learned on my uncle's farm / Robert J. Wicks.
    p. cm.
  ISBN-13: 978-1-933495-27-9 (hbk.)
  ISBN-10: 1-933495-27-8 (hbk.)
  1. Contentment. 2. Conduct of life. I. Title.
  BJ1533.C7W53 2011
  170'.44--dc23
2011018091

Some people are fortunate and content enough with life that they seem to relish almost every moment. When such a person is also a fine scholar and educator, society benefits in many ways as well. And, when this rare type of individual also turns out to be my closest friend and laughs at my quips, even better!

In memory of Joseph W. Ciarrocchi (1944–2000)— thank you for being such a gracious and faithful soul.

Is there a quiet stream

underneath the fluctuating affirmations
*   and rejections*

of my little world?

Is there a still point where my life is
*   anchored*

and from which I can reach out

with hope and courage and confidence?

Henri J.M. Nouwen
The Genesee Diary

CONTENTS

_____

LIFE *is* SIMPLER
THAN WE MAKE IT

Children have a great sense of simplicity. It can be so refreshing. Adults, on the other hand, can often and easily get lost in life. Writer and physician Walker Percy put the issue quite well in his novel *The Second Coming* when one of his characters asks, "Is it possible for people to miss their lives in the same way one misses a plane?" That quote has haunted me since I first heard it. It pulled me into my past and allowed me to recognize and name experiences that were beneficial to me when I was quite young. Without my being aware of it at the time, these experiences laid the groundwork that would later help me respond to, and even avoid, the danger of missing my own life.

Each June as a child, I would leave Queens in New York City and spend the entire summer on a family farm in the Catskill Mountains. Originally run by my grandfather and Uncle Tony, it was now owned by my father and two uncles. Although not active anymore, the buckboard wagon and barn stood as reminders of a different time, a simpler life. Across the road, my mother's uncle Mike and aunt Anna also had a farm—this one still active and bustling with summer help and the presence of boarders eager to escape the New York City heat and stress for a little while.

During those years I didn't think much about the impact this time away from the city was having on me. Yet, later in life I would return to work and live in "the country" as we called it. After graduation from Fairfield University I went to live just a few miles from where the farm still stands, before I entered military service during the Vietnam War era. Following my discharge from the military and education for a doctorate in psychology from Hahnemann Medical College and Hospital in Philadelphia, I joined the staff of a hospital in Lancaster County, Pennsylvania, and worked as well in a rural clinic amid the Amish.

Even now I can see my present choices affected by what I consider to be my country roots. I now live in a small three-bedroom house made of local stone and red cedar shipped from rural western Canada. I jokingly describe it as a large stone fireplace (which is twenty feet high) surrounded by a small house. It sits on an acre of land parceled out from an old Maryland farm and has a small pond in the back.

The land is dotted with the gardens and trees I planted to keep me and my family company. They detoxify not only the surrounding physical air but the psychological space as well. At least, I feel calmer when I walk amid them or through the acres of forest of Patuxent River State Park, a short drive from my home.

Now in the fourth decade of my clinical practice, I can look back and realize how a country psychology has formed what I believe, how I think, and the way I live my life. It has helped both me and those who have come to me to find or regain a healthier sense of perspective in order to live a more meaningful and satisfying life.

Life is simpler than we make it. Knowing this can encourage us to focus more directly on what is truly important and essential in life. Adopting a psychology, philosophy, or spirituality that supports and fleshes out this way of living can be learned. And that is what the following pages are about.

I have sought to provide brief, poignant, sometimes humorous, and instructive lessons I have learned about the simple cornerstones of a life well lived. They are not new. I don't do "new." Yet, each of these principles and practices are worth dusting off and taking to heart, especially in today's world.

Media theorist Marshall McLuhan once questioned, "If the temperature of the bath rises one degree every ten minutes, how will the bather know when to scream?" I don't think we know when to scream today. The views of modern society have gone astray from early values and understandings that helped us respect ourselves and our community. We have also strayed from the reality that we have such a short time on this earth and should seek to live our fleeting days with meaning, peace, compassion, and contentment.

William James, the father of American psychology, believed that an action leads to a habit, a habit leads to the development of one's character, and a character leads to a destiny. Taking action with the right attitude or psychology as a guide can change our destiny for the better. It provides a more powerful lens to see more clearly the streams of contentment that come with living a more meaningful and simple life as well as the ability to share this experience with others.

What follows is a distillation of the principles that I learned long ago, have honed over the years, and have practiced with myself and my patients. Take some time with each chapter and ask yourself, "How can I absorb this principle? What ways am I practicing it now? And, how can I practice this even more deeply so it becomes a part and fruit of my ethos?"

An Invitation to Take the Second Risk

As a youngster raised in the city, I learned about the need to be all that I could be in life. I was told to expand my horizons, be willing to risk failure by reaching higher and higher. Rejection had to be faced. Accepting what was "a sure bet" was not good enough.

Given my personality I responded to this challenge even though I felt failure keenly. I remember trying my hand at writing a weekly column in high school (all copies of which I now hope have been burned.) Other steps of this process of risking included becoming a Marine Corps officer, marrying someone I felt was much more spiritually mature than I was, applying to a doctoral program that I knew was going to accept only seven candidates out of the 360 who applied, writing books for respected publishers, going into Cambodia to work with persons trying to help the Khmer people rebuild their country after years of terror and torture, and working with physicians, nurses, and psychologists treating returning, critically injured military personnel at Walter Reed Army Hospital. As I look back I see that I did take the risk to be who I could be. I did deal with failure upon failure on this road even though I felt it deeply since I am so thin-skinned. However, I now realize that taking the risk to be in over my head and not settle for less, is not—as I thought it was in the past—the most important risk I would need to take to live fully.

The road now involves taking a much more subtle and somehow more demanding risk. The question which haunts me now is not what *more* do I need to do to be satisfied with my life. Instead, the second, more profound, countercultural risk is to appreciate who and what is *already* there in my life. The greater, more crucial calling for me now is to be content with who and where I already am. Not to do so would be to miss so much with which I have been graced.

Whereas I learned to appreciate the first risk in the intense competitive environment of New York City, the seeds of how to approach the second risk were planted in the country. I experienced in the rural people a different pace of life each summer and a style of living that many of us in the city might consider as quite basic and unworthy of any real gratitude or excitement. Eating a hot breakfast, doing the hard work baling hay and moving it into the barn, running to see a cow's calving process that went off without a problem, falling asleep while sitting under a tree watching the sun set, or enjoying a glass of homemade hard cider on a Friday evening with family and friends from another farm are only a few of the available gifts that we valued in the country. Quite possibly they would be "no big deal" to others.

I also felt this difference on one of my trips to lecture in Newfoundland as I drove around the little picturesque town of Corner Brook in the western part of this most eastern province of Canada. As I drove along the ocean and took in the tough landscape that survived the sometimes brutal winters, I felt a peace. I had a sense of knowing that the movements of the seasons didn't just mean a change in clothes but that life was something beautiful, if only I had the eyes to appreciate the gifts of each season. I needed to learn again and again the value of looking out the window in the morning and seeing what is—not moaning about what it could or should be.

During my summers spent on the farm in Liberty, New York, I explored our seventy-eight acres of forest and open fields and went down to the stream to look for crayfish. I caught a glimpse of a woodchuck popping its head out of its hole and then waddling off to find food. Deer moved by me in the early mornings; crows would make themselves known overhead. It was good spending part of my growing up time this way, and I think it helped me take in the simple rural spirit, to learn elements of a country psychology that in later years I would see described in various, yet somehow similar, ways by spiritual writers and in books on gratefulness and mindfulness. I had been given it all here. I had been presented with the lens of simplicity and contentment early in life; now I just had to know when to periodically pick it up again. I think I have done this in many conscious ways, and my desire with this book is to share these experiences and the principles that I learned from them with you no matter where you physically live.

I.

—

Lessons *and* Stories *on* Uncovering Fresh Streams *of* Contentment *in* Your Life

one

―――

KNOW WHO *you* CAN *be* NOW

In my experience, many people who live in rural areas often seem to be more "real." On the other hand, those of us raised in urban areas (like me) are often taught to put up a front for the people we are with. We are told to play a role, keep our defenses up, stay safe. Adding to the deception, although no one says it explicitly, we are advised—especially beginning in adolescence for males—to inflate our ego. Yet, when we do this, we start to value the wrong things and fail to grasp the implications of this role-playing. A famous quip by the writer Flannery O'Connor serves as a warning to us. When a friend complimented her on the publication of her book *A Good Man Is Hard to Find*, she wrote back saying that fame was merely "a comic distinction shared with Roy Rogers' horse and Miss Watermelon of 1955."

We sacrifice a great deal in being so concerned about our reputation and persona. All the energy we spend on our defenses and building up our egos (because we were told, and erroneously now believe, we are not good enough) is not available for creativity, growth, and appreciation of who we *really* are. (I know someone who has played so many roles that I don't think she knows who she really is.) However, we eventually see the folly of this masquerade if we are fortunate enough to interact with persons who model transparency and self-acceptance. This is reassuring and surprising—and often quite enjoyable. True ordinariness is, indeed, a tangible wonder.

I remember once visiting a hermit who was so non-defensive and at ease with himself that I don't think I aged when I was with him. After all, how could I? Aging takes some sort of friction. There was none. If for some reason I would have verbally attacked him with a statement like, "You are a fool!" I don't think he would have defended himself. Instead, he would have paused, reflected (rather than reacted), and responded with a smile, saying, "Yes, I do behave foolishly at times, but how did you know?"

Another person who stood out for me like that was Jack, a Lutheran pastor who was a professional counselor, educator, and my department chair at the university. Nevertheless, he for me typified the image of a country parson. He was gentle, welcoming, wise, and had a look in his eye that was either compassionate or full of fun depending on the circumstances.

Jack was also typical of the country parson in how he meticulously minded the funds. And so I was shocked when he said to me one morning that we should go out to eat together on the department to mark his passing of the leadership torch to me. He said, "Bob, soon you will be chair of our department, and I will be moving back to faculty. I think it is justified that we take money from the budget and go out to eat."

I was incredulous. "You mean we are going to go out for dinner together on the department, Jack?" He calmly replied, "No, *lunch,* Bob, *lunch.*"

We did finally match our schedules and went out. After we had a chance to look over the menus and order, I asked Jack to say grace before we began eating as a nod to his role as minister. He agreed, bowed his head, and belted out a prayer of thanksgiving. Everyone in the restaurant put their knives and forks down. There was a couple in the corner that I think were planning to have an affair. They changed their minds! Finally, he looked up, smiled, and said, "Well, I think we thanked the Lord well enough."

That's the way Jack was. He was spontaneously himself. He knew who he was, enjoyed himself fully in being that person, and all of those with him were touched by his comfortable honesty as well. His ordinariness was magnetic.

This is different from people who *think* they are ordinary, transparent, or spontaneous, but are instead erratic, leave no psychological space for others, or are just plain rude. I had a colleague in graduate school many years ago like that. His unconscious was close to his mouth. He thought he was simply being himself when he would blurt out uncharitable comments, but instead he was actually living out a role that was unexamined and unnatural. It was more a reaction to his family of origin than to the people in front of him.

Poor fellow. I think he was trying to be like another of our classmates who also said outrageous things but was so likeable and fun that he would make you laugh rather than react. I still remember one day when this other classmate came up to me, stared at a flamboyant tie I was wearing during my rotation on the inpatient psychiatric unit, and quietly said, "Where did you get that tie?" After I told him, he said, "Do me a favor. Don't go in that store again."

He was impossible, but the special thing about him was you always knew he was kind and liked you. Ordinariness and kindness make a good combination. When people are their spontaneous, gentle selves—no matter what personality style the person is clothed in—everyone around them feels good as well. You feel cleansed by their presence, much like when you take a quiet walk in the woods.

Gentleness warms our style of interacting with others so the best of our personality can come forth. This is especially so when we turn that kindness on ourselves so we can see clearly, but not hurtfully, what our faults are and what our gifts can be. It doesn't take much to be this way, just a little attention and effort. And when it happens, not only do others feel the difference, but so do we.

Yet ordinariness seems so rare today. There are so many people who are self-centered and narcissistic. Once, a colleague of mine gave a workshop on psychiatric diagnosis to a large group of mostly female social workers. As part of the presentation he showed little video clips of the different psychological disorders. When he was showing one of a narcissistic male, he noticed that in the far back of the room six of the social workers were giggling loudly. When the lights came up, he had to ask them what their observations were and why it was so funny. In response, one of them yelled out, "All six of us dated him!"

To be truly our ordinary selves, each of us must respond to three calls. If we don't, there is a good chance that we will spend our lives focused externally on our persona or reputation, merely existing, drifting, or reacting to the events. You might ask, "Don't many people live that way?" Yes, I think they do. When a certain spiritual guide was asked what he learned after years of mentoring others, he responded sadly, "Most people are unhappy, and they make the same mistakes over and over again." But we don't have to live that way. If we are aware of the three calls of identity each of us must face eventually in life, we can let go of the past and respond to the calls when they present themselves.

Answer your three calls.

The first call is: *self-awareness (*or what I like to call knowing your "true name"). There is more in a name than we realize until we come upon the use of one that opens our eyes. We especially see the importance of names in the Bible. In the Hebrew scriptures, Abram is called to become Abraham, the father of his people, and Sarai to become Sarah, a woman filled with new potential. In the Christian scriptures, we see how Simon is renamed Peter, and later Saul becomes Paul. Our given name often brings with it the limits family and society have put on it. Our family role quietly and unconsciously follows us into adult life like an invisible puppeteer. However, if we determine a name that *we* believe is truly reflective of our gifts, then we have a basis for discovering what it might mean not only for us but also for those with whom we interact and whom we guide.

I remember years ago saying to my wife, "I have a new name." She is used to these types of crazy proclamations from me, so she simply replied, "What is it?" I said, "Enthusiasm." She paused and looked at me. "I don't like it." I told her that this wasn't meant to be a sharing; it was more of a male thing. I wanted to simply utter it and have her applaud. Finally, realizing she was right, after a bit of reflection I said, "What about 'passion'?" She smiled and said, "I like that one. It is large enough—it is *you*."

I then began to see how I could feed the name "passion" that I felt captured my main gift. I wanted to do this so it could be pushed into the realm of magic for myself and others whom I served as therapist, friend, family member, coworker, or associate. Via my passion I sought to bring whatever natural joy I could into all situations. I wanted to encourage people. I also wanted to learn how I might inspire them in my presentations and writings. The goal was to honor passion as I lived it out in my own life. I knew this would take work, but that it would be well worth it. And, I must say, I was pleased with the results. I did find that by using this new word or name as a guide, I could really live out a meaningful life. But after some years I ran into a wall. I was being called now to respond to a second, less direct calling in life: *pruning*.

I began to see that I didn't need to take any further steps to extend my central talent but instead needed to prune it. I needed to take an even more difficult step than I had in the past: I needed to step *backward* into the shadow or the underused areas of my psyche and find a new name or word to balance "passion." If I didn't, I would be intrusive in people's lives. My passion had become irritating rather than enhancing for others. It had become unfocused and unruly, like an untended rose bush. In seeking this balancing word I came across the word "gentle" as a guide. I needed to be a gentle passionate person. The gentleness would be like the greens around the rose. It wouldn't supplant my main gift but would accent it in such a way that it could be better appreciated by me and of more use to others.

This worked quite well. It produced the same results that we see in nature when a bush or tree is properly pruned at the right time: more fruit is produced! I could see that when I was more attuned to when and how to intervene with others, I could have a greater impact than when I just passionately pushed ahead full speed. The same is evident with other styles/names/words as well. For instance, if you are a great listener and this is your main gift or name, then there comes a time when listening must be pruned in the direction of activity. Choosing to sit at the far end of the table is no longer humility; it is unnecessary diffidence that results in the loss of your presence from the community you are in. One friend told me that she naturally was an introvert and that she tended to listen and not participate in class. Unlike extroverts who speak first and then think, she thought before speaking. The result was that she reflected a great deal, but didn't share. Finally, her teacher said, "I recognize your listening style, and it usually is of great benefit to you and to those with whom you share your ideas later on. However, to remain with this style now in class is actually selfish; you need to risk sharing your thoughts with your classmates even though they may not be completely formed in your mind." I asked her what was the result of this comment by her teacher. She said she was surprised but thought it was a helpful encouragement at that juncture, and she did start to participate more. She knew that she needed to prune her old style with a new one at this particular stage in her life.

For many people, I think this stage represents most of our adult lives. We are spontaneously ourselves when we step up and balance our names as our ordinary way of dealing with the world. However, there comes a time when both self-knowledge (finding your name) and pruning are no longer sufficient. It is at this point that we are called to a final stage: *transformation*.

Transformation takes place not when we push ourselves forward or take steps back into our psyche. At this stage growthful steps won't do. Something else more dramatic is needed. One spiritual master's question to his disciple illustrates this. He asked his disciple how he was progressing. The disciple replied that he was making advances by taking little steps. The master, knowing transformation was necessary at this stage in his disciple's life, responded "You can't cross a chasm by taking little steps. You must leap!"

The leap is called for when we no longer feel that balancing our first word (in my case, "passion") with a second word (for me, "gentle") is sufficient. Instead we are called to take a leap to embrace the most mysterious step of all (transformation), and to do this we must be willing to live out the rest of our lives by making our second word our first word.

A movement such as this will require a great deal of mindfulness. We will need to live in the now with our eyes wide open to life. Such attentiveness can only come when we have spent sufficient time in response to the previous two calls. If we don't have enough self-awareness to realize how important it is to balance our central *charism* or gift, it just won't work. That is why we shouldn't seek to move too quickly. There is no advantage to attempting fast advancement through the three callings. Rushing can even serve to hold us back. We will be merely paying lip service to our calling and failing to see that we are not living up to it.

People often ask what the reaction of others will be when this leap is taken. If it is taken at the appropriate time and done well, nothing. No one will notice, because the result will be subtle. People will sense that something about us is different but not know what it is. On the other hand, if it is not taken at the right time and in the right spirit, then we will be like the talk show host who yells the loudest when he knows the least. It will be all words, not a living expression of who we are.

The choice to respond to each calling when it comes is, of course, up to us. It is up to us to hear the sometimes quiet call to become who we are destined to be at that moment or stage and decide to answer it. This overall process is well described in a familiar Native American story called "The Two Wolves."

One evening, an old Cherokee told his grandson about a battle that goes on inside people. He said, "My son, the battle is between two wolves inside us all. One wolf is 'Evil.' It is anger, envy, jealousy, sorrow, regret, greed, arrogance, self-pity, guilt, resentment, inferiority, lies, false pride, and superiority. The other wolf is 'Good.' It is joy, peace, love, hope, serenity, humility, kindness, benevolence, empathy, generosity, truth, compassion, faith . . . and *contentment.*"

The grandson was amazed at this. You could see it in his face. You could also see that he was puzzling over what he had just been told. Finally, he could no longer restrain himself, so he asked, "Which wolf wins?"

The old Cherokee grandfather smiled slightly and softly replied, "The one you feed."

Contentment is enhanced when you recognize, respect, and respond to the calling of each phase of your life as it is revealed to you.

two

BE CLEAR ABOUT
WHAT *is* TRULY ESSENTIAL

Most people, if asked whether they could say what was critical in life and what wasn't, would probably answer in the affirmative. However, when I work with helping professionals such as physicians, nurses, psychologists, ministers, educators, social and relief workers, and others who are under great stress because of the delicate and demanding work they do every day, I try to get them to make further distinctions. Otherwise, they run the risk of burning out or acting out in unhealthy ways. These distinctions are, I think, important for everyone to make.

I refer to them as the "five categories of critical." (This is a modification and slight expansion of the groundbreaking work of Stephen Covey in his book *The 7 Habits of Highly Effective People*.) The categories include:

1. Very critical in life
2. Critical to us in the long run

3. Critical to others now
4. Not critical ever
5. Critical *not* to do

Very Critical in Life

What is *very critical in life* tends to be quite obvious on a farm. It might be something life threatening like when one of the young, summer farm workers from the city turns over a tractor on himself and is pinned under it. Or, it could be that one of the animals gets in trouble. I still remember the panic in my cousin's voice when her dog decided to investigate a porcupine passing through the property. In a frantic phone call she said to me, "He's got quills in his nose, Robert, and he is starting to foam at the mouth." I told her I would get help and be right over. There was no time to wait for the vet; it would take him forever to get there. I called my supervisor at the New York State Narcotic Addiction Control Commission, who lived nearby, hoping that as a part-time farmer himself he had dealt with this before.

He said of course he would help. He drove directly to my cousin's place, and we were both there in under half an hour. He said we must act immediately or it might end disastrously; the dog was suffering so much right before our eyes. My cousin and I held the dog, while my supervisor poured antiseptic over the dog's nose and quickly pulled the quills out one by one with a pliers. It was over in one minute.

Naturally, it would have been better to sedate the poor dog first, but there was no time to wait for the vet, and we could not think of an alternate plan. In any case, our intervention did the trick, and the dog lived for a long time after that. He had only one discernible post-traumatic response after this negative experience. From that day on, he completely lost interest in porcupines. Would that people could learn lessons that quickly.

Critical things in life are usually rare, extreme, and in need of immediate action. The danger, though, is that, like television shows hyping up no news as breaking news, we may be tempted to make things into crises that are not and do not need to be. When I took over as chairperson of the graduate program in which I still teach at Loyola University Maryland, I told the faculty that usually when a new person assumed leadership, it was best that he not make any immediate changes. I said that I agreed with that in principle, but I would make one change: there would be no more emergencies. They laughed because they knew what I was talking about. We had grown so rapidly that the department was constantly being overwhelmed with new challenges for which we hadn't prepared. So, when challenges occurred we erroneously saw them as crises that needed immediate action.

I explained using the metaphor of a store. We once were a little mom-and-pop operation. Then, we became a supermarket. Now, as the benchmark program in the world, at least four times bigger than the next program of its type, we were like a huge chain of stores. We would make lots of mistakes. As a matter of fact, if we weren't failing a lot, something was *wrong*! Statistically, the more you are involved, the more you fail. If you are not failing enough it means you are being too cautious and not creative enough to anticipate and participate in change. So, in the future, we should not see challenge or change as a crisis but rather as a call to adapt and deepen. Such a process usually takes time and reflection—not immediate mobilization.

I think I actually over-succeeded in this change because a few years later, the associate chair of the department came in with a true crisis. Typical for her, she had a well-prepared plan to deal with it and asked my reaction. When I offered a suggestion that included one minor change, she left my office and then quickly returned and stuck her head in the doorway. I noticed that this time she was smiling. I said, "What?" She replied, "You know I hate to admit it, but it has been so long since we have had a good crisis that it is sort of fun and energizing to finally have one to deal with again." And we both laughed.

Discern your five categories of "critical."

In all of our lives it is necessary to really discern what is truly critical so we don't become crisis junkies. Somehow in the city we learn to thrive on crisis and hyper-excitement so much that some newspapers and television stations see it as their mission to meet this need by looking around until they find trouble. The sad part of this is that people absorb this type of existence, begin to feel overwhelmed, look for magical solutions, and even feel bored and a bit depressed when there is no crisis in the offing. It is like we get up in the morning and tick off what we have to do and face until we finally come up with what we consider a serious problem. What a way to live or, more accurately, exist!

Critical to Us in the Long Run

The second category is *critical to us in the long run.* When working with physicians, nurses, psychologists, and others in the helping and healing professions, this is the one area that I emphasize. And, even though it is very crucial, it is the one that is most neglected. There are many reasons for this, but the most basic one is that we take the elements that are crucial for our well-being for granted or postpone them for the future. These elements include psychologically, physically, spiritually, and socially rewarding activities such as taking the time for relationships, renewing pursuits, silence and solitude, educational experiences, leisure, and exercise.

We tell ourselves that once something else is out of the way, then we'll take time for ourselves. But we are deluding ourselves because *then* rarely or never comes. Also, as Wayne and Mary Sotile point out to doctors in their very helpful book *The Resilient Physician,* when this category is not attended to, then the *very critical* category expands and fills in the space in our schedule we should have allotted for self-care. Life becomes a constant state of dealing with so-called crises. The question we must face is: What self-care program have I developed for myself, and how much time do I provide for it? (There is a full discussion of this in my book *Bounce: Living the Resilient Life* [Oxford University Press, 2010].)

Critical to Others Now

The third category is *critical to others now.* Whether they are our children, friends, coworkers, associates, or those who call us on the phone to solicit money or our business just as we sit down to eat, a whole array of people want our attention on their schedule. How we deal with that is up to us. I once knew a medical-school dean who had this message on his answering machine: "The missus and I are not home now. Leave your name and phone number, and if we like you, we'll call you back."

Setting limits for others is very important—not just for us, but for those we wish to reach out to in our interpersonal circle. If we go to every meeting, say yes to every request, expect ourselves to always perform at an "A" level, or feel that others must always come first, then we are setting ourselves up for a perversion or depletion of our caring energy.

It is important to have priorities and limits in the way we respond to others. If we are able to "prune" (using that key word again) our compassionate responses, then we won't be giving less to others, but—just as in nature—we will be blossoming more in the quality presence we offer others.

Not Critical Ever

The fourth category is *not critical ever.* In this we can include sharing our words but not ourselves (gossiping, elevator talk, or meaningless cocktail party stories), surfing the channels with no intention of enjoying a specific show, skimming through the newspaper as a way to fill time, and other mindless activities that don't renew us. It is amazing that we spend so much time doing such things when life is so short. We behave this way as a matter of course, without thinking about it. Once when I went to the fish store to get some freshly made shrimp salad, the proprietor said it would be ready in about fifteen minutes. I said, "Is there something to do in this area to kill the time until you have it ready?" His surprising response was, "Killing time. That's a terrible way to look at the open periods in your life." My first mental reaction to him was, "Oh, lighten up." But his words stayed with me. I was on automatic pilot and had a "Thank goodness it's Friday" mentality. In the process I was giving away most of my life. When category two (attending to what is critical to us in the long run by being involved in good relationships, sound self-care activities, mindfulness, etc.) is strong, this category of *not critical ever*, though still present, plays a much smaller role in our lives.

Critical Not *to Do*

The final category is *critical* not *to do*. Knowing about this category can be extremely useful because it can help us avoid costly mistakes in life. When I was at Hahnemann Medical College, one of the finest psychiatrists I had the pleasure to be taught by said in passing, "There are fantasies you should act on and ones you shouldn't. Knowing the difference between the two is crucial for your happiness." For some reason, and I am glad of it, I never forgot his words and must confess that anytime I have violated them I have paid dearly for it.

When I treat or mentor other helping professionals who have done something inappropriate in their work with patients, clients, parishioners, or colleagues (what we refer to as "boundary violations"), they often comment, "It just happened." I can understand this type of reasoning, but it is still a poor excuse. We must prepare ourselves for the dangers that arise in helping and healing others.

I remember once, after losing some money in the stock market on a fairly risky investment that had promised great returns, I realized that I was, in effect, gambling with my retirement money. This insight left me with a greater resolve to behave prudently. But I found that I was tempted to make the situation worse even after I realized my mistake.

I had bought 5,000 shares at $1.00 per share of a stock with a very impressive technical name without even figuring out what they did. Finally, after a number of months, I thought I should check back in with the broker and ask him what the firm's products or purpose were. He seemed hesitant and said, "I'll send you the prospectus." "No," I replied, "you can just tell me." He still refused, and when I received the material I could see why. The company had no actual products on the market—everything was in the development stage.

When I was done reading this, I called up the broker and asked him, "How much is this stock worth now?" He responded, "$8.27." I was momentarily elated. "Per share?"

"No. The whole 5,000 shares."

"Well, what do I do now?"

He replied, "Well, you could buy more and lower your initial cost." What's worse is that, for a few seconds, I actually considered doing this.

We are responsible for our lives. It is all right to take risks if we think them out. However, being rash or impulsive without reflection is not an indication of freedom or reasonable risk taking. It is just acting out and being irresponsible.

In the end, no matter how we might be tempted to blame others or the situation, *we* are the persons in charge of our own actions. That is why knowing about this fifth category (critical *not* to do) is crucial for our well-being and the well-being of our family and society.

We must be able to discern among the five categories of critical. Our lives are short. Our possibilities for enjoying and sharing our lives with others are great. In discerning between these categories and acting accordingly, we can then recognize what we are facing in life. We can diagnose the source of the challenges and joys before us, achieve an appreciation of how we can make life better or worse, take appropriate action, and then let go. It's as simple and as difficult as that. How and whether we do it is up to us.

Great inner strength and contentment are experienced when you discern the five categories of critical (especially category two) and take care of yourself. If you do this, you will have the energy and natural motivation to meet the crises and challenges that arise in your own life and in the lives of those who need your compassion and support.

three

─────

Practice *a* Little
Faithfulness

Driving down the Lincoln Highway on a sunny Sunday morning to make rounds at the hospital in Lancaster was normally a joy for me. In addition to patients in the psychiatric unit, there were some medical patients in intensive care or on other floors for whom we were providing consultant services, and I enjoyed the work a great deal. Moreover, the ride was usually relaxing since it was through Pennsylvania Dutch Country. However, this morning was different.

I had risen early thinking I didn't have duty that day. I had just started to drink a cup of coffee and was reading the Sunday *New York Times* in the den when the phone rang. It was the head of psychiatry, and he wanted to know whether I planned to go to the hospital to provide coverage this morning. (I could pick up some tension in his voice as he said this.) I told him that he hadn't mentioned it when we had office hours earlier this week, so I thought I was off. Then he told me in fairly colorful language (that wasn't psychiatric in nature) what he thought about my interpretation, summarily told me to get out there, and hung up.

After this jolt to my relaxing morning plans, I thought, "Well, maybe I can quickly get in and out and be back home with my coffee and the paper in a couple of hours." I encountered the first block to this short-lived fantasy toward the end of the drive to the hospital. As I was moving rather quickly down the highway, I spotted the dreaded orange triangle. This was the bright symbol affixed to the back of Amish buggies to warn the drivers behind them that they were going slowly. Very, very slowly.

To make it worse, he didn't turn off until we had practically reached the hospital. Finally I pulled into the doctor's parking lot, double stepped it up the stairs, and headed for the unit to see how many patients I would see. After nodding to the nurse at the station, I reviewed the list and saw there were only three names on it. Yesssssssssss!

At the start of my rounds, I visited a young Amish boy who had been in an accident. He looked a bit frightened, and I wound up doing most of the talking. Keeping a relaxed look, I sat down and chatted as if I had all day, in the hope that I could put him at ease with me and his situation. After being there awhile, I stood up and said, "I'll stop back again to see you before I leave," and I smiled. He looked up and said, "Ok." My thought was as I left him, "Poor kid. He's still scared from the trauma of the accident."

When I moved on to see the other patients, thoughts of the young boy faded from my mind. Our encounter had slipped my mind so much that when I finished the last visit,

I went out to my car, forgetting my promise to return before leaving. Suddenly, just as I was getting in the car, I remembered him. At first I thought, "He probably won't remember and didn't seem to get much out of the encounter, so I can skip it." Then, after a few seconds of vacillation as to what I should do, I slowly closed and locked the door and returned to the hospital.

When I entered the room, I said, "I'll bet you thought I had forgotten you." In response, he looked up, smiled at the recognition of a now-familiar face in this strange environment for him, and said, "No, I *knew* you'd come back." His comment and the small pained smile on his face made me see how we often don't see our impact on other people and the potential joy present in even brief, passing encounters.

Gestures of kindness can be more important than you think.

This little epiphany was something important to remember; it was both simple and profound. I could let it go as a nice but fleeting experience of meeting someone in need, or I could see it as a beacon shining on such temporary meetings with others. It demonstrated to me how important these little happenstance moments of faithfulness on my part could be if only I recognized and appreciated their deep value—even if the results did not seem immediate or great.

The significance of small moments was reinforced for me by a simple story from a collection by William Bausch. The pastor of a small church received an envelope marked, "Please give to Harry the usher." The pastor put it in his pocket and didn't think much about it until he came across Harry on Sunday and then remembered to retrieve it for him.

The pastor stayed with the usher while he read the letter. Then, with tears in his eyes, Harry handed the letter to the priest, who read:

Dear Harry,

I'm sorry I don't know your last name, but then you don't know mine either. I'm Gert, Gert at the ten o'clock Mass every Sunday. I'm writing to ask you a favor. I don't know the priests too well, but somehow feel close to you. I don't know how you got to know my first name, but every Sunday morning you smile and greet me by name, and we exchange a few words: how bad the weather is, how much you like my hat, and how I am late on a particular Sunday. I just wanted to say thank you for taking the time to remember an old woman, for the smiles, for your consideration, for your thoughtfulness.

Now for the favor. I am dying, Harry. My husband has been dead for sixteen years, and the kids are scattered. It is very important to me that when they bring me to church for the last time, you will be there to say, "Hello, Gert. Good to see you." If you are there, Harry, I will feel assured that your warm hospitality will be duplicated in my new home in heaven.

With love and gratitude,
Gert

We never know the impact our little acts of warmth and kindness will have. After all, think of how much "small" kind gestures by others have meant to you in the past—especially when you were going through a tough patch in your life. Sometimes we want to retreat from small acts of friendship because we believe we can't do anything. For instance, people often say to me, "I didn't do anything for him. I *just* listened." We don't realize what "just listening" can do for people. Even though I am in the listening business, I still didn't realize how important it could be for others until one of my patients set me straight on this, years ago.

When I started my clinical practice, twice a week I had a long day. I started at eight o'clock in the morning and wouldn't finish until nine at night. (Thank goodness I don't do that anymore!) This particular day I received a call at noon during a short break for a snack. It was a patient I had seen for about six months, and we had, at least in my estimation, made good progress. He said that he wanted to come in to see me to process something that just happened. I said, "Is it an emergency, Jim?" "No, doc, it's not, but I would really like to talk about it *today*. I don't want to lose the energy I have around it. It's important to me."

I responded, "Jim, I have a very full day. You deserve to be heard when I am full of energy. Besides, the earliest I could see you would be 9:00 p.m."

"Great," he replied. "I'll take it. See you then," and he hung up.

My dismay was not just because it would lengthen an already long day. Part of it, I knew, was my inflated ego. During the therapy, I had made what I felt were truly insightful comments. (I thought that even Freud would have to go some to top me in this instance.) I was worried that given my lack of energy, I would not be able to measure up to my past intervention. To make it worse, when he finally did come in, I was even more tired than I had predicted. I thought, "He is going to be really disappointed." I don't even think I had the energy to say "hmm" convincingly enough when he made a point.

Well, it didn't seem to matter to him. He jumped in with great energy to tell his story in a way I seek to have all my patients tell their stories. He described the event as objectively as he could and also shared his subjective response to it. Then he pointed out ways he could have lessened the negative impact on himself and opened up avenues for using the insight he was gleaning from the event and his feelings and thoughts about it. He noted that this could ultimately change any distorted beliefs and improve his actions and reactions in the future.

Finally, I looked at my watch, realized the time was just about up, and softly said, "Excuse me, Jim, our session is almost over." In response, he said, "Okay, but let me add just one more brief comment," and he did. After doing this, he stood up quickly and said, "Thanks, doc. I know you were very tired, and I appreciate your squeezing me in so late." He then shook my hand, went to the door, and then swiveled around. "You know what, doc?" "No," I said. "I think this is the *best* session we have ever had!" he announced to me, smiling. So much for my brilliant interpretations and my being Sigmund Freud Junior!

Even in our family and close circle of friends, having the right attitude and a willingness to listen can make a big difference. Ever since I was little, my brothers and I were aware that our aunt, my mom's only sibling, didn't work or go out much. During the summer she would always say she was coming to visit us while we were at the farm, but she would rarely come. Often she would cancel at the last moment, and my mom would say, "Her bags were packed, but she wasn't well enough to go." After this happened year in and year out, we would tease Mom by saying, when we heard she canceled again, "Were her bags packed?" Mom, used to raising three boys, would make a face and say, "You just don't understand."

Later in life, I did begin to understand that my aunt was phobic, and my mom felt caught in the middle and wanted to protect her. She was very faithful in this regard, and finally I realized that the best thing I could do was simply listen to Mom's comments about why her sister couldn't do this or that. As a matter of fact, even though some of the conversations seemed surreal at times, listening seemed to help my mother feel understood, which I felt was all she wanted in these circumstances. Once when Mom was ninety-five years old, her sister—ninety-three at the time—was sitting beside her chatting with my wife. Mom leaned over to me and in a stage whisper that you could hear two floors down said, "You have no idea what your poor aunt has to deal with physically. Do you know what she is suffering from now?"

"No," I said in a whisper, as I leaned over toward my mother to hear what she wanted to tell me.

"Your aunt has a *gastric* stomach."

"No. Tell me she doesn't." I said with a serious expression on my face.

"Yes. She does. And there's more, too."

"No. What else?"

"She also has arthritis of the skull."

"Nooooooo. She really does?" (At this point, I had all I could do to keep a straight face.)

"Yes." And nodding and smiling knowingly, she leaned back satisfied that she had finally told someone who would listen, understand, and share this burden with her. Heaven knows what I would have said or how I would have reacted when I was younger and felt the need to do something. As we get older we begin to realize that sometimes *simply listening* is the best gift we can give to someone.

A little faithfulness, a willingness to listen, and a generous spirit: we can do so much for people if we are willing to be present to others with this threefold attitude, rather than merely waiting for "significant opportunities" to do what we feel would help. As a matter of fact, what makes us think that presence isn't even more important than the so-called "big" or valuable (to our minds) actions we would like to take?

Once, a Catholic nun working in Central America received a donation of $100 from a friend in the United States. She was thrilled with the gift and decided to use it to throw a party in one of the local parks for the poor children from the barrio. She rented a bus, had a tent put up, served ice cream, and had games for them to play. After the long day came to an end they all walked back to catch a ride home. Just before re-entering the bus, she asked the little girl she was walking with what she liked the best about the day. The little girl responded, "When you walked back to the bus with your arm around me." A little faithfulness can make a big difference.

Seeing what you can do and when you can do it, and then simply doing it—without concern about the size of the results—is no small gift to others. It is also a potentially powerful source of contentment for you. When faithfulness to, rather than success in, helping others is your primary goal you will avoid a great deal of unnecessary frustration if things don't turn out as you or others would like.

four

———

Don't Let Go . . . *Choose*!

I must have been a sight. That's what I think of when I reflect back on me at the age of twelve and in charge of getting the milk each week on the farm. No, I didn't have to milk the cows for it. (My uncle had already tried me on that. The end result was that everyone in the barn was practically on the floor laughing at my technique; that is, everyone but the cow, who was ready to kick me.) What I had to do was take a large, stainless steel pail, which weighed a ton, down to the shack across the way from the barn at the bottom of the hill to get it filled with milk from one of the cans sitting in "the cooler" (a cement trough filled with cold water). After one of the farmhands helped fill my pail, because the large three-foot milk can was too heavy for me, I had to haul the pail back up the hill. My mom or aunt would then pour it through paper strainers into individual bottles. There was obviously no pasteurization going on, but all of us lived through it.

In the morning I would then check the bottles in the refrigerator to see if the cream had risen to the top in each of them. What I didn't understand the first time round was why they then shook up certain bottles and took the cream off the top of others. My aunt explained to me that they took the cream off some so they could use it for coffee, and they would have skim milk left over for cereal. The bottles they shook up would then be whole milk for a growing boy like me to drink with my sandwiches.

Since I hated skim milk at the time, I remember thinking that it was a shame we couldn't have both the cream and whole milk, because I liked them both. I didn't want to choose. I wanted it all. Not so surprising for a twelve-year-old, but it's not so good for an adult to think this way—though unfortunately most of us do at times.

I thought of that experience years later when a young woman came in for treatment. She was tall, blond, and bustling with energy. There was something vivacious about her spirit. I knew right away that the therapy was going to be filled with intense interchanges, even before she got into anything.

As is my style, after I took down the usual information (spelling of name, address, phone number, date of birth, date of interview), I set the writing tablet down and asked, "How may I be of help?" She responded by telling me she was too forthcoming and impulsive in sharing her feelings and wanted to change that in herself because it was costing her too much. I asked her to give me an illustration.

"Well, recently I found out that my boyfriend was going out behind my back."

"Really? Behind your back?"

"Yes."

"With someone you *knew*?" (I wanted her to quickly get in touch with her strong feelings about it.)

"Yes. My younger sister."

"Your *sister*? I don't believe it!" (I wanted to encourage her to express fully how she felt.)

"Yes. I was furious."

"Well what did you do about it?"

"I called my boyfriend and let him have it."

"I'll bet you did. What did you say to him?"

With great energy, she then related how she had told him off, using some very colorful language. (I must confess I hadn't heard those words put together quite like that before. Very creative.)

"Then what did you do?"

"I slammed the phone down on him!"

"I'm sure you did. That must have felt wonderfully freeing."

"Yes. It did."

I then paused and said softly, "And you want to give that up?"

She then became quiet and sad, and finally said, "But after that we never spoke again."

At that point I remember taking off my glasses, pausing again, and saying, "Well, unfortunately as much as we obviously would prefer it, the tough part is we can't have it both ways. We can either have the pleasure of letting out steam whenever and wherever we want and take the consequences, or we need to be willing to postpone our actions until we can think through how we want to handle the problem. We need to make a choice on which 'benefit' to let go."

Letting go of behaviors is similar to letting go of things. It is not easy. The poet Donald Hall has suggested that instead of saying "Live Free or Die," New Hampshire's license plate should read, "It might come in handy." Letting go is difficult for many of us. Yet it can determine whether we can be in control of how we interact with others and also whether we have to remain chained to bad things that happen to us.

Experience more freedom each day.

My uncle Mike had a great way of handling things when he was upset. He would face them, share his upset, and then move on. I remember, for instance, the time someone let the air out of his tractor's tires up on the farm. This was not only an inconvenience but it was very costly. Because the tires were so large, you needed to have someone come out to your place to re-inflate them. Uncle Mike noticed the flattened tires early in the morning, and you could see he was upset. He couldn't take the wagon out to pick up the hay as he had planned, and rain was in the forecast. Rain would ruin the recently cut hay, and it couldn't then be stored in the silo for the cows. But he didn't say anything more about it until the evening. Then he sat down with the group of us as his audience and related the whole story of what he had discovered in detail and why he was upset about it. Then he stood up, said three expletives in a staccato-like fashion, and went to bed. It was done. He had felt, shared, and let it go. I always admired that style in him and have tried to emulate him when upset.

Letting go is vital because it enables us to move on as we should in a challenging situation. I remember learning this lesson in the military. When I was in officer's training school, I was confronted with something called "the confidence course." It was an incredible feeling when I walked up in front of it and saw what was before us. I remember saying to the fellow dressed like a boy scout who was our drill instructor: "I don't think I can do it. Why don't I just go around it and set up some tables and beverages for you and the boys." He said, "What?!" and then he bent down and whispered something in my ear. I can't really share with you what he said, but to give you a flavor of it my response was, "Is what you just suggested anatomically possible?" He replied, "If you don't do it, I am going to personally show you." I responded by saying, "You know, I don't know where it is coming from, but I am feeling new motivation welling up in me."

As I progressed toward the middle of the course, I spied what I assessed to be a very simple obstacle. It was an A-frame made of wood with a rope hanging from it and a ditch underneath the rope. The drill instructor modeled how to traverse the obstacle. He simply ran up to the A-frame, grabbed the rope, swung over the ditch, and let go. When I saw him do it so effortlessly I thought to myself, "I have misjudged these Marines. Here is an obstacle to build up our confidence so we don't get discouraged." But just as I was thinking this, I noticed that the Marines in front of me were swinging over . . . and swinging back! Or they would swing over, and just as they touched their feet on the ground they would lose their balance and have to grab the rope to save themselves. Most missed and fell into the ditch.

I then thought to myself, "What is the difficulty in doing this? He did it so easily." Then it hit me. There was only one way to get beyond this obstacle successfully. You had to run as fast as you could, grab the rope, swing over, and while in midair *let go*. If you waited until your feet touched the ground, it was too late. You couldn't have the security of touching ground before letting go. You needed to trust yourself and let go in midair before sensing the ground support you as you normally wanted or felt you needed.

Letting go, first and foremost, involves making a choice. It is choosing what we want to happen. It is seeking something new and good rather than merely focusing on what we have to let go of. This is how we move ahead. Freedom comes with not being possessed by everything we feel we need. But the desire to move ahead often requires a leap into the darkness.

As one alcoholic shared with me when I asked him how it felt to stop drinking: "It is not about what I am losing; it is about the full life ahead of me that I am now opening for myself by not drinking anymore." In other words, he was saying quite directly that the focus was on a new choice to experience the many flowers in the garden of his life rather than to be captured by just one. Whether the motivation is dissatisfaction with impulsive behavior or basement clutter or is a desire to cross to a new land on the other side of life's ditches and obstacles, the process of letting go can only succeed when we trust ourselves with a focus on the new choice and what it can bring to our lives. Once again, letting go is a lesson in life that is simple yet hard to practice. It is also a lesson that would do us all good to remember and emulate, especially when we come up against the call to *let go*.

Exchanging the rewards of old styles of behavior for the fresh freedom and contentment that comes from living life fully now is indeed a great trade-off . . . if you have the courage and motivation to do it.

five

APPRECIATE MORE FULLY
EVERYTHING *and* EVERYONE *in*
YOUR LIFE NOW

After a rather surprisingly wet and cool July, August began with a muggy day close to one hundred degrees. By eight in the evening it had cooled down enough for me to take a short walk down to the large pond that sat at the bottom of the hill.

First, I stopped at the small horse farm next door to lean over the fence and enjoy the colts running around the pasture, trying out their no-longer spindly legs. It was exhilarating to see them and also funny because they hadn't quite gotten the gallop down yet.

Then, as I walked further along I spotted a deer trying to blend in under a tree while eyeing me with a gaze that said, "I'm invisible, right?" In response, I waved to him and kept on going so he could stay where he was, eating some berries that had fallen to the ground. As I moved beyond the edge of a high hedge grove, there, lying on the gravel road leading to a house hidden way in the back, was an impressive red fox.

He lifted his body and trotted off after he spotted me. But it wasn't so fast that I couldn't size him up as a strong, full adult, certain to intimidate his future prey.

It was a lucky evening walk. I love seeing nature in action up close. Yet just as I returned home and got inside, thunder and lightning struck with a burst of rain. It tore in half a large maple I had planted years ago down by the main road. It also completely toppled a twenty-foot blue spruce next to the house. Luckily the tree fell away from the house. Otherwise, who knows what damage it might have caused?

The storm's suddenness and ferocity startled me into remembering the fragility of life, which had started to move to the recesses of my daily awareness. It always does when I don't consciously remember a simple, poignant reality: I am dying and everyone else is as well. People often react with a sense that I am being morbid when I share this thought. But am I? Don't we appreciate others' value to us and the brevity of our own life when we make friends with the reality of impermanence and the fragility of life?

Michel de Montaigne, in his *Selected Essays,* tells the story of a tribe in Africa that used to place a skull on the table during a party to remind all present of their finitude. This was not done to put a blanket over the joy but to have people respect this enjoyable time they had together in community.

At an educational event on mindfulness cosponsored by Harvard Medical School, Mark Epstein, who has written extensively on both psychotherapy and Zen, related a story on impermanence and the fragility of life. It was originally told by the revered Buddhist master Ajahn Chah to a group of psychiatrists visiting him in Thailand. Before they

Let fragility soften your soul.

were to leave, he held up a glass and said, "You see this glass. I love it. It holds water, and you can drink from it. If you hold it up to the sun, the light shines beautifully through it. And if you ping it with your finger," and he did, "it makes a wonderful sound." Then after a pause, he smiled and said, "Then the wind comes in through the window, blows it over, and breaks it. *Of course.* And because I know this about this glass, I love it even more." Knowing about our fragility can wake us up to enjoy life as never before.

One of my counseling students, who also had a practice as a massage therapist, demonstrated this to me in a story about one of the persons who came to see her. When she was seeing this client, whom we shall call Carol, the two of them began to speak about the client's recent bout with cancer. In the midst of the surgery, chemotherapy, and radiation treatments, Carol's friends would often say, "Won't you be glad when you can get back to your old life?" The massage therapist asked her, "How do you respond?" Carol smiled and said, "I tell them, 'Oh, no, that kind of life is just what made me sick.'" She then went on, the therapist told me, to become a nurse, the profession she had always wanted to follow but felt she couldn't for all kinds of reasons she no longer considered valid. Fragility, whether we encounter it in a dramatic way or recall it through some small happenstance during the day, can truly wake us up—*if* we are willing to recognize and accept its lesson.

Once I was called to the hospital to meet with a woman who had had a miscarriage in the final trimester of her pregnancy. When I asked her what specifically about this loss bothered her, she replied, "When I think of the son or daughter I have lost, the one point I find most painful is that I shall never know who my child was or what he or she would be like. Would he have been a hyperactive boy, or would she have been a quiet little girl who didn't say much, but you knew she was planning something outrageous in her mind? I'll never know, and that is a special sadness for me."

We who do live, who have been born and who have a personality that can be known by us and shared with others in good ways, have a duty to let our personality evolve so others can benefit from who we can be. The fragility of life reminds us of this and helps us regain perspective when we are with others. Once born, everyone is beginning to die, and because of this everyone is worthy of love, even more than Ajahn Chah's glass. It is a good thing to remember when we are ready to say negative things about others or to judge ourselves harshly.

Being aware of our own fragility can also help us to be more compassionate when we are in helping roles. This is especially the case when we have gone through our own psychological and physical turmoil. I reflect on this especially in the case of my own daughter.

She had a particularly intense adolescence. Even the choice of some of her boyfriends was something to behold.

I remember sitting in the kitchen one evening in front of the greenhouse window. I watched with amazement as a young man in a very creative outfit walked in front of the window and up the stairs onto the front porch. Just as he was about to knock, I said to my wife, "Something just walked across the lawn, and I think it is trying to get into the house." To which my wife responded with a stern look and said, "Don't say anything to embarrass your daughter when I let him in." I responded, "I promise, if you just keep him off the hardwood floors."

I must admit, as I look back, that he was a very nice fellow as were most of the young men she dated. However, as my daughter's own two daughters approach the teen years, I remind her that, as recompense for her teen years, I plan to set up a beach chair in front of her house and watch her interactions with them.

In addition to the normal challenges of adolescence, my daughter had serious physical problems that resulted in her having thirteen levels of her spine fused and a steel rod anchored to her spine for stability. This was followed in her university years by complications requiring the rod's removal by a specialist at the Johns Hopkins Hospital. Other chronic problems still plague her today.

Yet she has chosen to use all the psychological and physical experiences—which were sometimes quite extreme—and let them help her appreciate her husband, her children, her parents, and all of life. Her experiences have also enhanced her work as a Veterans Affairs social worker responsible for severely injured military personnel returning from Iraq and Afghanistan. She displays a positive attitude and welcomes each of them. One of them was so taken aback by her greeting that he said, "You certainly are up-beat." She responded, "You have served us, and now we are going to serve *you*. Come in and tell me what we can do for you at the VA." Is it any wonder that I am so proud of the woman she has become?

When you let your own fragility and experiences of trauma soften your soul, your attitude is passed on to those with whom you are in contact. I have seen this in my daughter's influence on her children.

One of my granddaughters, for instance, recently informed her mother at bedtime that during "circle time" at school that day she had prayed for her mother's friend. She then went on to say that she also was going to pray the next day for their cousin Ryan, who had recently been awarded the Purple Heart and Bronze Star with Valor in the Middle East. She then asked how he was doing, and my daughter explained that he was hurt but getting better. She replied, "Mama, I feel so lucky to have such a special cousin. I think his face should be put on a coin!" Out of the mouths of babes.

Experiencing the fragility of others and the way they deal with it can also be a teachable moment for us. Even working as professional helpers isn't simply a process of reaching down to people in need. It can be a circle of grace for the helper who has the eyes to see.

After the devastating earthquake in Haiti, a physician who is also a Catholic religious sister took a break from her work at Johns Hopkins and flew to Haiti to see what she could do to help. When she arrived she was assigned to work in pediatric emergency medicine since she was familiar with this specialty and they desperately needed assistance in this area.

One of the children she treated was a seventeen-year-old boy who had had a concrete wall fall on him. It crushed his pelvis and sent a metal bar through his upper leg as well as his privates and into his other leg. Once the bar was removed, he was naturally bedridden. The physician decided that it would be a good idea to involve the young man in some way since he was immobile and would benefit from both companionship and a new sense of purpose. As a result, she asked him to guard her duffle bag that held all her expensive "doctor's instruments," worth thousands of dollars. He agreed and took the job very seriously. Even when he was sleeping, he would curl his arms through the straps so no one could attempt to steal the bag without awakening him.

After being there for a while, the physician realized she was getting hungry. In the rush to leave she had only brought with her three bottles of water, which were almost gone, and a few bags of nuts. If she were to continue working twenty to twenty-two hours each day, she would need to eat something, so she thought of the nuts, took the bag out, and was getting ready to eat them when she realized the young boy was looking at her.

She felt she couldn't eat them while he also was obviously hungry, so she gave him a handful before she ate what was left. However, he didn't immediately eat them even though it was obvious that he was very hungry. Instead, he first gave half the nuts away to the girl in the next cot. In turn, she then split her portion in half and passed them on to the next child and so on until the child in the last cot received a few nuts to quell his hunger a bit as well.

Her lesson: *Learn to share.*

Another teachable moment for the physician came after she had to amputate the leg of a very young boy. She checked on him whenever possible to see if the dosage of narcotic she gave him was keeping his pain at bay. They had a signal between them: he would give the thumbs up if he was fine, and they would both smile.

On one of her visits to him, she had a rare chance to sit by his makeshift bed and chat. As she was doing this, a new bus of injured young children arrived. You could tell from the crying and screaming that there was a great deal of suffering, a great deal to be done. Before she could take leave of the young boy though, he looked up at her and said, "Go. I don't need you. *They* need you."

Her next lesson: *Even when you are suffering, never forget to care for others.*

Fragility has many lessons for us: life is precious, and if we are open to it, over time suffering can soften rather than harden us. Our greatest teachers can be people in pain, if we allow them to teach us.

Seek to let sadness soften your soul and help you to be more open to growth and new possibilities rather than to believe your only choice is remaining frozen in permanent discontent.

Bitterness need not be your permanent fate; the history of many persons who have undergone terrible tragedies but have gone on to live gentle, contented, and compassionate lives teaches us differently.

six

Know What *a* Renewing Community Really Is

One of the most enjoyable towns I have ever lived in is West Chester, Pennsylvania. It had interesting little shops. The places to eat ranged from a mom-and-pop place to a fine French restaurant to a spot with the best ribs in the area. Since it was also the county seat and a college town, you could always count on it to be bustling and filled with good energy.

The town also made it a point to celebrate everything, so you can imagine what it was like during the Christmas season. There was always a performance of *A Christmas Carol* and a person reading *A Child's Christmas in Wales* in a candlelit room somewhere in town. Of course, Santa traveled down the main street in a horse-drawn sleigh, waving to us all.

There was also a group of carolers, and I was once roped into being part of it. I don't have a good voice, and inflicting it on others wasn't my idea of a Christmas gift from me to the community. However, after some cajoling and a glass of Swedish glogg, it seemed like a good idea. Well, as we moved around the town singing, I thought to myself, "I'm not half bad!" Then the woman next to me who had a sterling voice stopped in the middle of one of the carols to clear her throat, and I could hear myself singing "Joy to the World." I couldn't wait until she started singing with us again.

When we are part of a community, life is so much better and more balanced. In many parts of America, we don't often live this way. But in rural areas we need friends to help us make it through the year. My uncle Mike would often call on one of his friends to help him quickly bale his hay when it looked like a storm was brewing. He didn't have a baler—just like I didn't have a singing voice!—but knew he could count on someone else who was able to quickly get his hay into the barn. Rural communities are like this the world over, though sometimes what they encounter is much more dramatic and can be a sharp reminder to us that we can't and shouldn't do it alone.

Strengthen the balance in your life.

Toward the end of the Zimbabwean war of liberation in 1979, when one of my counseling students was six years of age, a fierce battle was fought in the student's small village. He was alone with his four-year-old brother. The battle raged for the whole day, and people were scattered all over the village. About half of all the children in his village died, including his close friends. For a day after the battle, he and his brother were unaccounted for and were presumed to have died with the rest.

Then they were found hidden in a house where they had somehow survived the gunfire and aerial bombs that had destroyed much of their village. Children who had taken cover in similar places had perished, but they had made it. My student told me that, as a professional counselor looking back on the event, the impression the community made on him even surpassed the horror of the violence. When I asked him about this, he said, "We spent a great deal of time afterward telling the story of our survival. I believe it is this retelling of our story and the attention of so many people that helped us to integrate and mitigate the trauma. The village provided an environment for mourning those who had died and for healing those who had survived. Communal ritual practices played a very important part in cleansing the land and the people at the end of the war. I learned to have a great respect and admiration for the leaders of these rituals and the people of the village, and this was not the last time that they were to come to my rescue."

When I asked him about that, he told me that when he was ten years old he got trapped in a burning hut that he had accidentally set on fire. The fire had started at the only entrance to the hut, and the flames were too much for him to go through. He felt this was his end and let out a wild scream. Fortunately for him, his father braved the inferno and got him out. He had lost consciousness due to the heat, smoke, and possibly fear.

When he finally regained consciousness, he was lying in a room surrounded by the women of his village, who were nursing his burns and offering him food. He could also hear the voices of the men outside and knew that the whole village had come to support him and his family.

Two weeks later, he told me, the village elders came to his home to perform a ritual partially intended to prevent similar accidents, but also—and of even more importance to him as he looks back on it—to help him deal normally with fire.

To accomplish this, they built a model hut in the open field and instructed him to go in the hut and set it on fire in the same way as in the accident. They had him reenact the accident three times, and each time one of the villagers would rush in to rescue him. In addition, they had him tell his story again and again to village members who came to see him and his family.

From this he learned as a child something that people in rural areas seem to teach each other instinctively: namely, that the tragedy of one individual or one family is a tragedy for the whole community. This is a lesson from a country psychology that would be worth absorbing for all of us, no matter where we live. In the words of South African poet Mzwakhe Mbuli in his Zulu poem:

> An injury to the head,
> Is an injury to the whole person,
> Is an injury to the whole family,
> Is an injury to the compound,
> Is an injury to the village,
> Is an injury to the kingdom,
> Is an injury to the world.

No one who connects with a healthy community is ever bereft of the chance to both give and receive love. This is, indeed, a rich stream of contentment in our lives.

seven

BEWARE
the TYRANNY *of* HOPE

Lillian Carter, the mother of president Jimmy Carter, once said, "There are times when I look around at my children and think, 'I should have remained a virgin!'" Everyone gets discouraged by some situations they find themselves in—no matter how sturdy and accomplished the person may be.

Everyone experiences frustration, upset, and even personal darkness. At those times, it may be difficult to hope. When people are in a dark psychological space or a "spiritual hallway," they naturally assume that the whole house is dark. It is at those very times when they must have patience and hope.

Monk, contemplative, and spiritual writer Thomas Merton was walking past the infirmary in his monastery. He noticed an elderly monk sitting down, looking dejected. He approached him and asked how he was doing. The monk looked up and shared that he felt he was losing his spirit.

In response, Merton put his hand on the monk's shoulder, smiled, and said, "Brother, courage comes and goes. Hold on for the next supply."

When we were primarily an agrarian society, the different times of the year were appreciated more deeply and naturally—a time to plant, a time to gather, and even a time to let the fields lay fallow. Pacing, timing, and a realistic sense of what is possible with ourselves and others are all important to learn and regain. In his fascinating and sometimes enigmatic novel *The Shadow of the Wind,* novelist Carlos Ruiz Zafón writes, "Sometimes we think people are like lottery tickets, that they're there to make our most absurd dreams come true." When we deal with people close to us who are having problems, we need to have low expectations and high hopes so that we can greet them openly and freely.

In marriage counseling, for example, it is important to help the partners discern and share with each other the differences among basic needs, expectations, and desires. When these are confused, conflict can cause suffering that greater clarity could have prevented. To expect something (no matter how good it may be) of someone who is totally incapable of it can be very frustrating for everyone involved. As the old saying goes, "Don't try to teach a pig to sing. It irritates the teacher and frustrates the heck out of the pig."

On the journey that led me to become a psychologist, two friends and fellow students showed me important lessons. As I recall them, I go back to what one of my professors taught me about a key element of real treatment that I now see—many years later—as "a tyranny of hope." One of the friends was a male, the other a female.

The male friend was enjoyable to be with in many ways. He was gregarious, funny, insightful, and a hard worker. However, his view of the darkness of the world was pure projection. The message I heard between the lines was clear. He was never at fault and never had a role in his own problems. Instead, in his vacillation between depression and hostility, it was always someone "out there" causing his problems or misunderstanding him.

The female friend was also talented and hardworking. She too was brilliant in her assessment of other people's faults and shortcomings. Looking back, I am still amazed at her ability to accurately pick up this information. But due to her style of viewing the world, she would then make the mistake of taking the issues of others and personalizing them. For instance, central among their problems was a lack of appreciation for her and a tendency to let her down. In addition, she had this fascinating aversion to being grateful for what these persons actually did for her. Even when they praised or congratulated her for her wonderful accomplishments, she almost never said, "Thank you." It was as if saying thank you would cost her something.

Eventually, these two extremely gifted people puzzled me so much that I asked one of my professors who didn't know them about what I had observed. He was hesitant to respond since he didn't know them personally and, in his own words, "did not want to go on a psychoanalytic safari without any firsthand information." However, since I was so baffled, I pushed him for guesses. He finally smiled and said, "Sit down." (Now I knew I would hear something interesting.)

He thought a bit, looked at me, and said, "People develop a private logic early in life. It is the result of heredity and early childhood formation—in other words, the fit between the child and the significant adults that surround them. In the case of both your friends, there is a real fear of being wrong—to them admitting a mistake or having less than pure motives would be tantamount to admitting they are wrong as persons. If you confront them with what you see, even though it may be with an appreciation of their gifts and a desire for them to improve, they will feel threatened to the core. They will get angry, feel hurt, or say you don't understand. The expectation you have—that they look at themselves to see what they can discover that is negative or blocking growth—is unrealistic. Also, the fact that they can't see any of this means this style is totally beyond their level of awareness. What we call 'unconscious.'"

> *Call people to be all they can be without embarrassing them for being where they are.*

"Your male friend seems like an angry fellow—fearing he is not getting enough recognition, money, respect, whatever. In the case of your female friend, it sounds like she is afraid of abandonment. Something happened to her early in life and this music is still playing. So either you are with her or against her; there is no middle ground."

I replied, "But I like them both, and I wish I could help them see both themselves and the world more accurately.

They would enjoy themselves more and not be so hurtful to others. It would be a win-win."

"So it would seem," he responded. "As a matter of fact, that is what we do as clinical psychologists. Specifically, we help people relax with a combination of gentleness and clarity, and we then summarize patterns so they can refocus and decide what to do about any unproductive way of perceiving and acting."

"What if they refuse?" I challenged.

"Well, they often do. Your goal as a helper is encouragement and clarity, not forcing. Your goal is to be personally and professionally faithful to the process of helping people sit with the truth; success is nice, but it is not the goal. As a matter of fact, your having such a difficulty with these two people not seeing things as you do may be a problem coming out of your private logic; namely, forcing and controlling others, albeit for good."

"*Me?*"

He didn't respond to that but smiled and said, "This being intrigued with yourself is great fun, isn't it?"

Then before I left he added, "Psychiatrist Carl Jung once said, 'The brighter the light, the deeper the darkness.' You see, our gifts are really connected to our growing edges or defenses. So if you desire to help others lead better lives, then when you feel frustrated with them you may forget pacing and be intrusive. Instead of helping, you merely annoy them. Helpers need to look at their own defensiveness and feelings of frustration in sessions with their patients or clients. Their feelings can teach them about themselves as well as the persons they are trying to help. The fact we are speaking so intently about these two friends might mean that their problems are longstanding and so beyond their awareness that they are impervious to intervention. In psychology we call such problems personality or character disorders. It also might mean your need to get your way at the speed you would prefer is getting in the way of the help or treatment you wish to give. Worth thinking about." He then smiled, got up, and thanked me for our time together.

Although I still make this same mistake again and again, I feel I am better able to pick it up more quickly now. I seek to be more sensitive to it when I teach or supervise other clinicians. Failing to take the time to see how mature and insightful a person is before setting our goals and just trying to force that person away from dysfunctional thinking or unhelpful behavior, is actually an example of a *tyranny of hope*. We feel we are being kind, pastoral, therapeutic—call it what you will. But just like a stony field could never support certain crops, no matter how much we hope it would, certain people will never attain certain goals, no matter how beautiful they are in other ways or how much we wish they could. Knowing this doesn't mean we have to give up on our friends, family, acquaintances, or those we are called on to help. Rather, it helps us to be more helpful because we understand how to be with them in the best way possible given who they are. Now that is a real win-win situation!

Have low expectations of what you feel people ought to do and high hopes of the good they might do, and all of you may be pleasantly surprised; at the very least, you won't become disappointed, discouraged, or discontent if the results you wished for don't materialize in members of your family, friends, or coworkers.

eight

DON'T BE FOOLED
BY THE WINTERS OF
YOUR LIFE ... *Lean Back*

A friend told me a little story she heard when on a personal retreat in Tipperary, Ireland. It seems a young child (six or seven) asked her mother, "Where did the first people come from?" In response, her mom told her the story of Adam and Eve and their posterity. The little girl loved the story and seemed quite satisfied.

A week later, as children will do, she asked the same question again but of her dad this time. In response he went into great details about a particular kind of monkey-like creature which gradually became more human and then resulted in the human race.

The child became bewildered at this, so she went back to her mother and told her what her father had said. Her mother responded reassuringly, "Oh, don't worry about that. Dad was just explaining about his side of the family!"

How we perceive things is very important, and maintaining a healthy perspective—especially when we are in the heat of emotion—requires that we "lean back" a bit so we don't react without reflection. To act quickly is critical in an emergency; to do it in other situations may well be disastrous.

Once a young mother came to see me at a rural clinic. When she came in I was trying to recall the advice of a wise psychiatric supervisor who had extensive experience in working in rural clinics. He said, "Bob, they are not looking for the treatment provided by Sigmund Freud or Carl Rogers. They want someone to hear them out, diagnose their problem, break it down in a way they can understand, and then give them a prescription for what they need to do about it. It is different from the style of treatment we provide at our office on Rittenhouse Square in Center City, Philadelphia."

So after greeting her and putting her at ease, I asked her what I could do for her. At this she sighed and stretched out her long legs. She was a very tall young woman, so they almost touched mine given the small consultation room we were in. Finally after a long pause, she spoke almost inaudibly, "I want you to help me stop beating my kid."

I leaned back and assumed a relaxed position to put her at ease as well, since she was clearly upset about what she had just shared. I said, "Well, I can see you would like to change that behavior, so let's put our heads together and set up a plan of action. But first let me ask you a few questions. When you say you beat your kid, what do you mean?"

"Well three times in the past month I hit him once in the rear end, but I felt like doing worse, and I didn't want it to get to that. That would be bad."

"You sound like you know that from experience. Were you beaten as a child?" (In most cases, when people provide physical punishment to their children, it happened to them, and I wanted to see how bad it was.)

"Yes. Really beaten. He would hit me in the head until my ears would ring. My face looked a mess."

"So you haven't done that yet to your son, and you don't want it to get to that stage. What has your husband said about this to you?"

"He doesn't know. He isn't around too much, because he is busy coppin'."

"You mean he is a police officer?"

"Yes."

As I was questioning her, I began to formulate a plan so that she would be able to recognize when she was getting upset and distance herself from the situation until she could calm down. I knew I wouldn't be able to do much more for now, but that would break the cycle of spanking and prevent further progress to the type of violence she experienced at her father's hands.

"Well, let's do two things: one, help you to become more sensitive to when you are getting hot and angry with your son, and two, ask what ritual or steps you need to take to avoid striking out at him in the way you experienced when you were a child. It is good you want to break this cycle so your son will be less likely to follow in your father's footsteps and beat his children."

"Can I stop?"

"Oh yes, no problem. If you follow what I say, then it will work. If for some reason it doesn't work as well as you'd like, I'll recalibrate the steps I plan to give you." (I used a word that sounded technical on purpose to emphasize the scientific approach I was taking. The approach was behaviorally sound, although I would not be providing her with the reasons behind what I was doing.)

"First, I want you to observe when you feel yourself getting angry at your son. You will notice that your teeth are clenched" (and I made a face showing that), "your hands may be in fists, you start yelling at him louder and louder, and you probably are saying to yourself, 'I hope he doesn't continue this, because I am going to lose control.' Is that pretty much what happens, or is there something different?"

"No. That's it, but I also slam my fist on the table or a piece of furniture to let him know I mean business."

"Good. Well, when one of those things happens— especially the fist pounding—then take step two."

"What's that?"

"You need to change the temperature in your body because you are heating up and you need to cool down. So go into the bathroom, lock the door so your son can't rush in, run the cold water, take your watch off so it doesn't get wet," (I was trying to buy some time for her to calm down which taking off her watch would do), "and wash your face in cold water. Then dry your hands and face and put your watch back on."

"Is that it?"

"No. I also want you to keep a little writing pad or spiral-bound notebook in the bathroom. After you put your watch back on, write in it a note to yourself about how you felt when you were beaten and how you are happy that you are not doing the same to your son. After completing this minor ritual and leaving the bathroom, if you find yourself getting angry again, just repeat the process. Also, when you come in next week, I will have a little booklet, prepared by a specialist, to help you understand a bit more about disciplining children. Would you be up to reading it?"

"Yes."

"Well, then let's write all this down and make an appointment for next week." I then took a prescription pad and put down the steps for her, smiled, asked if there was anything else, and sent her off.

She came back the following week, and I could see by the smile on her face that she got through the week without spanking her son. She did need to use the exercise once, but it worked all right so she was pleased, but still anxious.

I took the time to ask her about her life, her marriage, and being a mother. Since I had already read the book I gave her (written by a child psychologist I knew) I went through it a bit before I gave her the copy. I then ripped off another Rx sheet and wrote several steps she needed to take to improve her own self-care approach. I only saw her once more and then asked her to call me if she needed more help.

This example shows how important it is for all of us to step back from our emotions. The opposite of detachment is not involvement with others, but rather the dangerous behavior of becoming overwhelmed. As a matter of fact, when we are aware of the feelings we have and can lean back so we are not consumed by them, we can become better friends, parents, adults, children, coworkers, or even therapists.

I remember once a priest called me and asked if I would see one of his parishioners immediately. Normally he referred people who had simple adjustment problems, so I wasn't even hesitant to squeeze him in at the end of the day, since the priest seemed to be anxious that I see him as soon as possible.

When I went out to the office, I found a 6'4" man, about twenty years old, waiting to see me. I introduced myself, brought him into the office, took the usual information, and asked, "Well, what seems to be the problem?"

When we enter "the cold hallways" of life, it is natural to think the whole house is freezing.

His response was, "I have an irresistible urge to throttle my sister."

My immediate inner reaction was, "With a problem like that you ought to go see someone!" Then I realized he had—it was *me*.

When I feel a strong emotion like this in the room, I know that to some extent I have caught it from the patient, so I responded, "This must be very overwhelming for you."

After he replied that it was, I asked him to tell me all about it. As he told his story, I was able to piece together the trigger for this surprising impulse and the underlying personality style that set the stage for it. After about eight sessions, he was able to see the logic of the impulse, which practically eliminated it, and to gain insight into his own tense style of relating, which he then addressed in some basic ways.

Emotion is the flag. Find out what dysfunctional thinking and beliefs are leading to the emotion, correct them, and the flag stops waving. Emotions are our friends here because they alert us to what needs attention—in ourselves as well as in those we seek to reach out to at home, at work, and in the larger community. Once again, the lesson is to lean back so that you can give yourself time to find or regain a healthy perspective. This is evident in the following poignant story by a spiritual mentor from Ireland who was once a student of mine. I close with it because it is my favorite story to illustrate this point, and it demonstrates once again the simple lessons that persons living in rural settings have to teach all of us.

> During what was a troubled time for me (I was about seven or eight) I visited with my aunt on her small farm. We walked together and came to a particular field. It was winter and frost covered the land. The ground beneath our feet was winter dark and hard.
>
> She looked over at me, smiled, and asked me to kneel down, close my eyes, and place my hands on the earth. I did so, and she said in a deep whisper, "Feel the life." I couldn't feel anything and told her so. She then told me to put my ear close to the earth and whispered hoarsely again, "Listen to the life." In response I put my head close to the earth and listened intently. But I heard nothing.
>
> When I got up and told her that I could neither feel nor hear "the life," she took my face between her hands and said, "*Alanna mo chroi* (child of my heart), it is often when the land seems most barren, cold, and dark that life is quietly growing!" When she said that, I knew she was also speaking to my inner pain and the need for hope during the winter I was experiencing at such a young age. Then,

almost as an afterthought, she added as we turned to leave, "We will return again in the spring."

And when spring came, we did return. As we came over the hill and I ran down the hill ahead of her, I could see that new tender life was shooting up. When she caught up to me, I turned to her and said, "You were right. You told me the truth!" In reply, she said nothing, just smiled, looked into my eyes, and drew out a smile from within my soul.

We also came again when the fruits of the soil were gathered. In this visit she spoke of the fact that this was the season of gathering the nourishment needed for the next winter, and she said, "Remember, *alanna*, to read the seasons. New possibilities, God, are in them all!"

The friendship this young Irish girl had with her aunt helped her to lean back during a "winter" in her life in order to read the seasons and see their possibilities. It also demonstrates the role relationships play in helping us to keep a sense of perspective. We have heard it said again and again, but it is easy to forget: we can't do it alone.

Patience (leaning back emotionally), friendship, and openness can help you sit with the personal darkness of anger or sadness until it softens your soul and teaches all the lessons of contentment that it can.

nine

WHEN *in* TROUBLE,
FIRST GET *the* DETAILS

When a veterinarian had to be called to the farm it was a big deal. My uncle liked to treat his animals himself for two reasons: after thirty years he felt he was practically a vet, and veterinary treatment was an expense he would avoid at all cost. As a child, when I heard that a vet was coming I tried to be outside the barn near an open window so I could eavesdrop. I loved to listen to the questions the vet would ask, and though I couldn't make much of it, one of the questions he always asked my uncle turned out to be one that my own psychiatric supervisor would check to see if I asked my patients: When and how did this problem begin?

One of the earliest cases I presented as part of my clinical rotation was of a very bright dental student who was depressed. The presentation was to my small cohort of six other therapists in training and the senior analyst. As is the custom, I was ready to discuss the case and then present an excerpt I had taped from the session. The analyst changed the pattern and said, "No. Just play the tape of the initial session first so we can get a sense of your style and the patient's presenting complaint."

I played the tape, and it sounded something like a bouncing ball:

Patient: "I feel depressed."

Me: "You seem down."

Patient: "Yes, I am blue."

Me: "You feel you are in the dumps."

After about ten minutes of this, the supervisor motioned for me to stop the tape. When I did, he smiled and said, "I don't think I have ever heard such an example of non-directive, reflective therapy."

Being my usual dense self even back then, I thought it was a compliment, so I thanked him.

He responded then by saying, "I did have a question though. When did you plan to begin the treatment?" (I could feel the rest of my classmates shifting away from me. I guess they thought to themselves, "No sense in going down with him.")

"I did begin the treatment," I said in a defensive voice.

"Well, why didn't you ask the patient *when* she became depressed?"

I wasn't letting go, so I said, "She's always been depressed."

"Well, when did she get worse?"

"She's always been this bad." (I wasn't backing down.)

"Well, why did she come into the clinic?"

"A friend recommended it."

"So, why did she accept her friend's recommendation at this point in her life?" Finally I had no answer to this.

After a pause, he said, "If you want to shoot the bull, go elsewhere, doctor. Get the details. Find the beginning. Because if you can find the beginning, you not only discover some sense of the cause, you put the patient at ease. If there is a beginning, then the patient will know that an end to her psychological pain might also be possible."

Finally, one of my classmates chimed in by saying to the training analyst, "You make it look easy, doctor; I am sure I would have made the same mistake as Bob."

At this point, the supervisor laughed and said, "I'd better be able to make it look easy after thirty years of practice. I also know Bob from working with him on the hospital floor, so I felt at ease teasing him. However, the serious point I do wish to make is that it is important to trace the problem as a way of plotting the solution. Otherwise, psychological treatment becomes simply a place where a person talks but nothing else occurs. This makes no sense given all we know about personality, psychological disorders, and the impact of the environment to improve or lessen a condition."

> *Surfacing the negative is a good initial step toward new emotional freedom.*

This early and beneficial encounter was the first of many with this analyst and other senior colleagues that made me realize why psychotherapy is really "an old person's game." To become wise in facing troubles in life requires openness and a willingness to see that there are key elements a professional must know about treatment. His comment about how long it had taken him to learn the art would later on ring true when I read a saying from the fourth century by an *abba* (sage or father) of the Egyptian desert. The abba advised someone trying to learn about living wisely that an important element was *pacing*. He said, "Don't try to understand everything—take on board as much as you can and try to make it work for you. Then the things that are hidden will be made clearer to you." I think that is also good advice for us as parents, colleagues, siblings, and friends.

Discernment about what we should do has often been compared to traveling to a destination at night. In the country where there are no street lights and people tend to limit how many lights they have on after dark as a way to save money, you can't see very far in front of you. A car's headlights allow you to see a reasonable distance ahead as you drive. So you see a little, then you drive a little, until you reach your destination. Discernment follows a similar pattern. It is not simply deciding what to do and doing it all. Subsequent to an initial discernment and action, we get more to discern. So we discern a little, then we act a little, until we arrive at our destination.

When I supervise therapists or spiritual mentors in training, I advise them of the importance of pacing. I remind them that if they go too slow, the patient will be bored in the session. If they move too fast, then the person will experience unnecessary anxiety.

Often the overriding reason for poor pacing in a session is that the therapist's and the patient's goals are not the same. And that is true for all of us in life. We will not pace ourselves the right way in the right direction if we are not aware of how our goals differ from those of our parents, others who are significant to us, and maybe the culture at large.

This is why a simple psychology of change is counter-cultural and so valuable. It should not be centered on pacing our lives with goals that come from the people around us. Instead, common values must be viewed critically. Freedom is not freedom to choose from the largest, most costly selection possible, but freedom to choose wisely given our short life on this earth. Wealth isn't having the biggest retirement stash no matter what the stock market does. It is having or being interested in possessing the inner wisdom to live with greater contentment and compassion with what we *already* have—which is not exactly the message of any advertisement I've seen on television recently.

Freedom also requires us to surface, recognize, and release hurts we have received in life. When we feel upset over something, we must take time at some point in the day to reflect on our negative feelings. Once again, we need to get the details and ask ourselves, "What am I really reacting to in such a strong fashion?" Then once we recognize what the source of the upset is, we should allow our emotions to be expressed—even if this means yelling about it by ourselves or with a close friend. This is obviously preferable to burying our upset or suddenly exploding inappropriately at a time or in a place we will wish we hadn't.

To varnish over negative occurrences does nothing but push them down further in the psyche where they sit and act without our awareness. They must be allowed to rise and be open to examination and healing.

It is natural to be angry and hurt over mistreatment by the people in our lives. It's like grabbing a hot poker—it would be foolish not to yell, and yell loudly. Still, once we have owned the sadness and the time is right, we must let go and move on. In an extreme case, sexual abuse for example, the process may take years and require great patience on the part of the victim and those supporting him or her. Certainly, not moving on would be as foolish as continuing to hold onto the hot poker while yelling. It just doesn't make any sense.

Whether we like it or not, in the end we are the ones who have the main responsibility for ourselves and the possibility of living a truly sensitive adult life. This includes recognizing our challenges, seeking to understand them the best we can, and, with the support of a balanced circle of friends, embracing them as a way of living within the "givens" of our own life.

The limits and givens in our life are a reality. To deny such constraints is foolish. Still, despite these constraints, there is much before us, both in reality and in potential, which we are missing because of our unwillingness to let go. I think Dag Hammarskjöld, in his journal *Markings,* was correct when he said, "We are not permitted to choose the frame of our destiny. But what we put into it is ours."

Surfacing and recognizing our hurts are important first steps. Releasing them is quite another matter! People often say to me, "I'd love to let go, but I can't seem to do it. Can you suggest a way?"

I think this is a fair question. The practical suggestion I offer again and again is, "If you can't seem to let go of the hurts, then be with them in a new way. Being with what you can't seem to work through, or let go of, in a different way may be the best response you can make. Too often we try to conquer the feelings we don't like. And when we can't, we feel frustrated at our inability to work them through or let them go."

I often suggest to people that they make friends with their "shadows," that they sit down and metaphorically put what they can't let go of (a thought or feeling) on the table in front of them and dialogue with it. If we have feelings of insecurity or feel buffeted in some fashion, we can be open to this negative presence in our life instead of trying to ignore it or being tyrannized by it.

For instance, in my own case, if someone invites me to give a presentation and then for some reason or other cancels it, my reaction may be, "Oh, I feel rejected. I wonder if I said or did something wrong." Then I might be tempted to shrug it off even though it still vaguely bothers me. Or, I might be haunted by it and not be able to put it aside. I might also try to deal with it by thinking bad things about the person who was the trigger for this feeling. However, none of these steps is really helpful, nor do they make any psychological or spiritual sense.

On the other hand, if I recognize that I have a negative feeling, note that it is similar to ones I have had in the past, and am willing to dialogue with it, the negative force can be removed. So, in the example cited above, I could sit down and dialogue with my negative feeling in the following way:

Oh, so you are here again. I'm not surprised. Everywhere I go you seem to come along with me and wait for something to happen that I don't like. You try to make me feel unnecessary resentment, guilt, or shame.

Well, I am used to you. I know that my foolish self-doubt and resentment travel with me everywhere I go, but I also know that I have positive gifts and that I am loved. I know that my trust in these talents and love will always be with me. I must recognize that I have faults as well and that these faults are actually connected with my gifts—often an exaggeration of them. However, I am not going to let my resentments, doubts, and other faults stop me.

In the past I used to try to conquer or hide you from myself. It was like I was trying to lock you outside the house on the back deck. Yet, each time you would surface and come back, and I, in my self-condemnation and self-doubt, would give you an inordinately prominent place in the house of my life—the master bedroom, the living room. I'd dote on you and feed you a banquet.

Now I know you are part of me—like the chaff that grows beside the wheat—but I am only going to give you a little attention. Instead of so much room in my life and head, you will have a corner of the attic. Instead of a banquet I will give you only a sandwich, just a little carefully dedicated attention.

So, thank you for being here to remind me that with humility I can take knowledge and turn it into wisdom. Thank you for reminding me that perfection and goodness are not synonymous. And thank you for sitting here with me to remind me that this incident can help me to learn more about myself because it calls to mind my foibles. It also reminds me to renew my awareness and faith in my gifts and signature strengths as well.

When we learn how to befriend our negative feelings and to see beyond them to our true selves, we discover that we are, at the core, both talented and loveable. Unmasking the charlatan in ourselves is important for both psychological and spiritual reasons.

Once, when sitting with Abbot Flavian Burns of the Trappists (a cloistered community of Catholic religious men), we began to speak about Thomas Merton. Abbot Flavian said that Merton was very concerned with seeing the truth about himself. He went on to note that he believes that when we die we will see ourselves in a true light. He said Merton probably wasn't too surprised by what he saw. However, when most of us die, we will probably be chagrined at what we see. In response, I teased him, "Maybe the word 'chagrin' would aptly fit your response, but I have a feeling a stronger word will fit me when I die."

There is a Zen saying: "Face reality, and unwilled change will take place." If we are willing to see ourselves as we are—*both* gifts and growing edges—with a sense of equanimity, while holding onto the reality that we are and have been loved and are now loveable, then much effortless change will become possible.

Often we don't look at ourselves honestly, because we are fearful and anxious about what we will see. The question we need to ask ourselves is: Are we willing to risk seeing the truth about ourselves? Or, possibly more pointedly: How much lack of safety can we tolerate in our journey toward self-awareness and ultimate freedom?

If we don't look at ourselves honestly, much self-delusion can and will take place. Even if we are well read and traveled, our worldview can still be narrow. Even our good traits can get overemphasized and distorted because we get tied up in protecting our own egos, which is a poor motivation for our actions. As psychiatrist and author Robert Coles pointed out in one of his talks at Loyola University Maryland in the fall of 1993, "Drive and ambition are good; but they can, as in the case of Napoleon, put us in the middle of a Russian winter." When that happens, we need to stop, sit quietly, *get the details,* learn, and deepen. Not to do so is just plain foolish and can be unnecessarily hurtful to us in the long run, as well as to those who count on us for an accepting face, a loving act, and a place to rest their burdens and worries. Yes, even when we face our own pain, it is not just about us.

Face the pain and negative occurrences in your life directly, no matter how hard initially this may seem, because behind them are the new wisdom, tenderness, humility, and contentment you and others in your life wish to enjoy.

ten

—

STOP THINKING YOU ARE GRATEFUL ... *Then See What You Inherit*!

When I was spending summers in the country, my dad would try to come up on the weekends. Since he drove a truck all week and hated the idea of driving on his time off, he didn't own a car. He would catch a ride with my uncle Jack and they would usually arrive after I was already asleep.

On one of these weekends, though, my father came to my room and woke me up. I still remember the night light and him sitting on the bed smiling. He had in his hand what looked to be an off-white case about twenty inches long. It was really made of hard plastic, but at the time I thought it was made of ivory. He handed it to me and motioned for me to open it. Inside was a beautiful, dark-red, felt container and in it a beautiful musket. It was only a popgun which shot a cork that was attached by a string, but it remains in my memory as one of the most precious gifts I have ever received.

Surprisingly, when I was in my twenties and living just a few miles from my boyhood farm with an older couple on another farm, I would have a similar experience. I was suffering from a terrible cold and decided to take a nap. After a couple of hours in bed, I heard an almost inaudible knock at the door. When I said, "Come in," the woman who owned the house stuck her head in and said, "Are you up to having a hot cup of tea and a slice of homemade blueberry pie?" When I nodded yes, she closed the door, and I got dressed and went down to the kitchen. I remember sitting at that table, the tea warming me inside, and eating what I still think is the richest piece of blueberry pie I have ever had. Just like the surprise in childhood, this small gift gave me such a large experience of life that it makes me ask to this day, "What happens to such simple, powerful moments when we enjoy life to the fullest?"

Psychiatrist Gerald May, in his book *The Dark Night of the Soul* (the final book he wrote before he died), pointed out part of the answer to my question. He wrote, "To put it in more modern psychological terms, most of us become desensitized or habituated to the especially delicate experiences of life. Most of us live in a world of overstimulation and sensory overload. Without realizing it, we erect defenses against our own perceptions in order to avoid being overwhelmed. We find ourselves no longer appreciative of the subtle sensations, delicate fragrances, soft sounds, and exquisite feelings we enjoyed as children. Like addicts experiencing *tolerance*—the need for more and more drugs to sustain their effect—many of us find ourselves seeking increasingly powerful stimulation to keep our enjoyment and satisfaction going." He then encourages us to recover our innocence, as well as to reestablish perceptiveness and sensitivity, so that profound peace, exquisite joy, and the fullness of love may become possible again. But for that to happen we must stop deluding ourselves about an idea that isn't really true: that we are already grateful.

In addition, we also need to better appreciate the connection between gratefulness and asceticism. Kathleen Norris, in her book *Dakota: A Spiritual Geography,* describes this connection quite well. She writes, "The western plains now seem bountiful in their emptiness, offering solitude to grow. . . . Asceticism . . . [is] a way of surrendering to reduced circumstances in a manner that enhances the whole person. . . . It may be odd to think of living in Dakota as a luxury, but I'm well aware that ours is a privileged and endangered way of life, one that ironically only the poor may be able to afford."

This statement may seem surprising at first, but when one thinks about it for a while it becomes clear. For instance, Israeli economist Avner Offer, after his survey of the impact of affluence on both developed and developing countries, comments, "Affluence breeds impatience, and impatience undermines well-being." As philosopher Søren Kierkegaard also recognizes, "Most people pursue pleasure with such breathless haste that they hurry past it."

For some people, life seems such a chore that even when they have so much, they are so dramatic about anything negative that comes their way. It is like every third Tuesday is "dark night of the soul" day. They clearly have failed to embrace the axiom: contentment is not the fulfillment of what you want but the realization of what you already have.

Part of the reason for this lack of true gratefulness is a failure to realize the reality of impermanence and the danger of a habit- or anxiety-driven life. Impermanence helps us realize how fleeting life can be—no matter how idyllic the setting. When I traveled to Iowa to offer a series of lectures, I had just completed a number of consultations in very difficult urban settings. My unspoken feeling was, it will be good to be in a quiet, stress-free setting again. And in one sense I was right. As I flew in over the fields of crops and wooded areas, I could feel myself decompressing.

There is so much more for you already in your life.

Then over dinner my host said, "I suppose it would be good for you to have a briefing on the stress we've been experiencing, since helping people deal with psychological pressures is what you do." I must have shown surprise on my face because he smiled a bit ruefully and said, "Oh yes, it is beautiful out here in Iowa. The people have real spunk, and it is a great place to live and raise children. But even here in rural America we have had more than our share of stress recently. We have had floods that after they receded left many homes filled with mold. Following this, we had a series of brutal hailstorms that left crops flattened and destroyed. The ongoing recession has wreaked more than its share of financial woes on people who were living on so little in the first place. Finally, something quite tragic happened locally." At this point, he paused so that I could continue to absorb what he was telling me, and then he added, "Our most popular high school coach was senselessly murdered. It was like we lost a favorite brother or uncle. We are still trying to make sense of this in our quiet, friendly community."

Being "in the now" and aware of the true fragility of life—namely, that we are dying and everyone else is dying too—helps us be grateful. It helps us to appreciate the people around us and the "affluence" we already possess. We begin to recognize that when we want more and get it, what do we need then? More, of course. When we believe we need something different to be happy and actually get it, what does it become then? The same, of course. And, if we believe that we need something or someone perfect to be truly happy, we run the risk of wasting our whole lives lamenting and waiting for this illusion. The reality is that when we have a truly grateful heart, everything is ours already—whether we technically own it or not.

I used to get a kick out of one of my neighbors. I would be killing myself outside trying to make my property look good. The healthy part of this was that I enjoyed the exercise and the possibilities to be creative. I also got great joy sitting in a little screened-in area looking out at the beauty of the trees, bushes, pond, and various animals that visited the property each day. It was peaceful and encouraging for living a sane life in so many ways.

Yet, like all amateur landscapers, I would compare my outdoor display with the others in the neighborhood. This took some of the joy out of it and sometimes caused me to overdo it physically in an effort to produce what was just the right look.

Well, my elderly neighbor taught me a daily lesson in this regard. Each day he would pass by slowly on his walk and look over the fence and appreciate the work I had done. He would drink it in and enjoy the beauty of it all, and then walk on.

He wasn't into competition or ownership. It didn't seem to matter to him whether I worked hard or not, whether it was a better display of bushes and flowers than other neighbors had or not. It didn't even appear to bother him that I temporarily held title to the land. He enjoyed it as much as I did. As a matter of fact, a lot of the time, I think he enjoyed it more!

We miss so much of what life sets before us, and that is sad. Our minds are elsewhere on other potential possessions or desires. We miss the plate set in front of us. We are like people in a room filled with tasty Italian food, but we are busy looking for another cuisine while the food before us gets cold. Instead, if we were sensible, we would enjoy the Italian food (the present gifts in our life) now so we would know how to truly enjoy the other cuisines (different future gifts) later, if and when they arrive. Isn't it crazy that most of us are so concerned so much of the time about how many years we will be on this earth, but we are not even enjoying the year, month, week, day, *moment* we are living in right now?

Deep gratitude nourishes contentment by opening your eyes to the hidden, undeserved graces that show up each day. Most people are unfortunately oblivious to these graces because they have predetermined what will make them happy and are therefore closed to everything else that is set before them.

eleven

RECOGNIZE THAT *a* LITTLE SILENCE *and* SOLITUDE IS NO SMALL THING

Years ago, a United States senator was asked the question, "What is the greatest challenge facing the Senate today?" His simple, revealing answer was, "Not enough time to think." I agree with his assessment and feel it is applicable to all of us. However, I think an equally pressing challenge is at the other end of the spectrum: we think too much and experience too little of what is happening around us and in us. We are either in the silver casket of nostalgia or preoccupying ourselves with a future that might never happen. We regret, feel resentful, worry, or plot our future but fail to live it even when we get there. Instead, we start to consider our new future. On the other hand, having a sense of mindfulness keeps us in the present. We are in the now with an openness to everything that is happening around us.

I learned a bit about mindfulness as a youngster during one of my summers on the farm—only I didn't know that it was mindfulness at the time. This was probably a good thing. When we label things, we then step back from the actual experience we are having. I would wake up some mornings and lay half-asleep, smiling, while the new rising sun drenched me with light and warmth. Everything felt all right. The past didn't intrude on me, and as far as the future was concerned, it was summer. I had no place to go. I didn't think about it or care.

Without my realizing it, these moments were occasionally joined by two longtime friends: simplicity and gratitude. I could hear a small van in the distance and would pop up in bed and look out the window. It was the delivery truck going to Siegel's summer camp about a quarter mile from the farm. It jostled along down a long dirt road, and I could see clouds of dust being kicked up behind it for a long distance.

On Wednesdays each week the van would also briefly stop at our house to see if we wanted something. Although my mother and aunt were trustworthy and generous, children sometimes can't count on adults—even good ones—to do the right thing. So I bounded downstairs each Wednesday to ensure they did, saying "We need to remember to buy an Entenmann's cheese-filled coffee ring." I would say it with a formal voice so they could take in the gravity of the situation.

They would always feign surprise at my announcement. Their questions disturbed me and convinced me that it was a good thing I came down when I did: Was the delivery van really visiting the camp next door? Did I think the man had time to stop by us before returning to the store?

When the van did finally stop and the purchase was made, I felt like I had won an Olympic medal. I also knew this would lead to two joys: a piece of cake now and a chilled piece (which made the cheese inside even better) later. Simple needs, a piece of cake . . . gratefulness felt all through my body, a great time in life.

But this kind of worldview is slowly taken away from children. Needs become, or—more often than not—are made, larger. Things are taken for granted. Simplicity, gratefulness, and mindfulness fade and are labeled unrealistic and impractical. Great desires, anger, neediness, entitlement (sometimes garbed as social justice) show up as our new "friends."

Yet a little mindfulness, sometimes steeped in silence and solitude and made more intentional by meditation, can open up some new space for us to refresh ourselves again as we did as a child. Being childlike, not childish, becomes a real possibility.

I still experience joy when I feel the warmth of the sun or,

Taking out a few minutes a day alone, quietly wrapped in gratitude, can produce truly amazing results.

yes, eat another piece of cheese-filled coffee cake, or when I take time out to be grateful for all the simple joys I already have in my life that I am not enjoying to the fullest. The helpful past and the gracious present are joined together.

When I went fishing in the summer as a child, I would get up early, put on my old clothes, hat, and waders, and walk down to what we called the Briscoe Bridge, a couple of miles from the house. Young adolescent boys are often not given credit for observing the beauties of nature and relishing quiet, reflective times. But that is not true. I looked forward to these times by myself. To this day I can remember how when I was twelve, the early morning scene on the pond struck me when I stepped over the brush and broken tree limbs into the water's edge. I would cast out my line as far as I could and slowly let my eyes retrieve the beauty around me.

The summer sun was just rising, there was still a layer of morning fog on parts of the pond, the trees were rich with different shades of green leaves, occasionally a bass would jump out of the water in an attempt to snag a water bug for breakfast, and at intervals ducks would make their usual terrible splash landing, sending rings of water out to the shore.

Even now as I pass a newsstand in the airport and see a cover of *Field and Stream* or *Outdoor Life* with a picture of an early morning scene on a lake or pond, I smile and think, "I've been there. I *know* what it is like." That image will always be with me in my heart, and I am grateful for it as a reminder of what it means to be truly alive.

These youthful experiences of mindfulness—whether at Briscoe or sitting on a rock in the woods making believe it was the beginning of time and I was the only person in the world—I now see as experiences of meditation. As I look back I recognize that they contain many of the important elements of meditation.

- I sat with my back fairly straight and simply gazed at the scene a few feet in front of me.
- I was patient without knowing I was being patient—I was in no hurry to go anywhere.
- I didn't plan to experience anything in particular, so the result was that many times the fruits of this time alone were rich and deep.
- I didn't think to judge or entertain any thoughts about the past or make plans for the future—being twelve years old and off for the summer just was what it was.
- I wasn't interested in solving or producing anything.

These were just gentle times, when I was alone without feeling lonely. I was someone who didn't feel he had been anywhere he wanted to get away from or return to. Nor did I think much about the future—it seemed too far away as I sat there in the forest by the pond. Such experiences need not be restricted to childhood. All of us have such moments as adults. They are good memories. When they come back they are beacons showing us how we can live even more like that now, rather than simply being nostalgic experiences we put on the shelf and look wistfully at as if they can't happen again.

Two other memories of the impact of silence and solitude, this time during my adult years, carry me away from home. One was when I was in Alaska leading a group of Catholic priests on a week's retreat aimed at tapping into the spirit of psychology. The locale was Alyeska, just outside of Anchorage. Those attending were housed in the lodge, the site of the morning conferences, as well as in small individual chalets that dotted the area. I was in one of the smallest chalets. It had a single large room, bathroom, and small kitchen on the first floor and a loft bedroom accessible from the first floor by ladder. Just perfect for me alone.

I observed a morning ritual that I have practiced for some time, thanks to a suggestion years ago by spiritual writer and friend Henri Nouwen. It is a simple ritual that involves getting up early, reading a bit, and then just sitting in silence—usually with a cup of coffee warming my hands. However, that first day in Alaska when I opened the blinds on the large downstairs window, I could see a hanging glacier in the distance and realized at that moment I couldn't read first. There was no need for it. The sight was enough.

Each day in Alaska I would quietly sip my black coffee (there was no milk in the house) and relax with the spirit of the landscape and with gratitude for the time alone there. I felt like I was at the gates of heaven. This time opened my heart to all the beauty we have in life that we miss when we don't take out time in silence and solitude—no matter where we are. It also brought me back to another faraway place: Japan.

I had been asked to give a presentation in the south of Japan. I did this, and in gratitude they had arranged a visit to one of the holiest Shinto shrines, a shrine set among the trees in a lovely country-like setting. Its name was Ise Jingu. Of course I accepted this invitation; it proved to be a perfectly timed gift, coming after a busy trip to bustling Tokyo and Bangkok.

At the temple grounds I was accompanied by a teacher from America who would translate what the personal guide would be sharing with me about Ise Jingu. As it turned out, she had taught the guide's children when he was a forester, and now he was in charge of the shrine. Her familiarity with both the guide and the place told me that this would be a special treat.

We walked the temple grounds, and the guide pointed out many fascinating things. Finally, he stopped as we reached the center of a carefully carved, slightly arched bridge. He pointed down at the water and asked, "What do you see?" After a moment or two, I responded, "Water that is clear, cool, calm, and probably refreshing." He smiled, seemed pleased with my response, said "*Hai*" (yes), and then asked, "Now, what do you *hear*?"

I listened carefully and responded, "It sounds like a frog." He smiled again, paused for a few seconds, looked expectantly at me, and announced, "You will not hear this species of frog anywhere else on the temple grounds." "Why?" I asked. "Because this species of frog only stays near water that is as you described: clear, calm, and refreshing." He looked intently at me to see if I fully understood what he was really telling me. Then we walked on.

Since this was a Shinto shrine, brimming with a sense of animism, I knew we had not been speaking about water and frogs but about something larger, deeper. He had called upon me to appreciate the crucial impact of being near and within a place that is calm, clear, and refreshing: silence and solitude. Otherwise, how could I hear and understand myself—both my journey and the cul-de-sacs I might get lost in on the way?

Early in life during my summer wanderings through the fields, town, and forest, I learned that everyone needs some quiet time alone either outside or at home. Most of us rarely experience it. But it is essential—even for those of us with a pronounced extroverted side.

A winter storm may be nature's way of encouraging this. The roads are unplowed, schedules are canceled, and some unexpected free time appears without any prior planning. On one occasion such a storm resulted in my canceling a long-awaited and much-anticipated visit to speak in Budapest. I was elated. My soul was so tired that knowing that I would have a full week to meditate, reflect, relax, read, and do some writing was like receiving a great gift.

Maybe the time to slow down and be quiet comes in a different way to you. For instance, maybe you get a "touch of the flu" and decide to stay in bed to sleep lightly, do some reading, watch an old movie, or jot down notes in the journal you irregularly keep but like to have as a tool to remember the turns in your journey. Whatever happens during these occasions, though, all of us need some silence and time alone. We need to recognize the rhythms in our day, week, and year that make this possible and take advantage of them wherever we can.

On the farm in the late spring and summer, time to slow down comes at the end of a long day before falling asleep. There are longer periods too when winter shuts down the haying, the summer help and boarders are gone, and people go to bed early after taking care of the animals. The middle of the day is quiet, except for slowly attending to those little construction projects that couldn't be done in the heat and activity of summer, such as repairing the pig pen or doing a proper cleaning out of the outer buildings. But whether we live in the country, in the city, or near the city—like I do now on a small section of what was an old farm—the possibilities for living fully come to light when we take steps to be mindful in silence and solitude.

For Robert Lax, poet and best friend of Thomas Merton, living out a country psychology actually involved a move from New York City to the Greek Isles where he lived the last thirty years of his life. In his diary, reflecting on his move from New York City and his recent move from one Greek Isle to another one that he found more conducive to his work as a writer and his life, he wrote:

> Night seems lighter, less heavy here . . . the weight of people stirring around at night, the weight of their thoughts, the weight of their plans seem to create a physical pressure in the air about all the cities: creates, that is, a psychological pressure so strong that it seems tangible, physical, bears down like a weight on the shoulders.
>
> It would be hard to imagine a similar weight bearing down on so small an island. Being gathered even from the nocturnal fantasies . . . of so small a community. . . .
>
> For perhaps the same reason, an incident taking place (and I still mean at night) in the city has not the same weight as one that takes place in a smaller town; an anecdote told at night in the city doesn't

resonate quite like the same anecdote told in an island village. There are paradoxes to be discerned here, because although life in a city seems to be constantly changing, each violent occurrence within it, each brutal fact seems to be permanent, seems to become part of its unchanging face; in an island village the opposite is true: the hills about it are permanent. The seasons come and go in a stable rhythm; houses are built to stand till they fall; children carry the names of their forebears, and, within this mostly cosmic framework, incidents in the life of man seem smaller, more ephemeral: parts, rather, of a cosmic pattern than isolated omens of good or ill.

As a result, a country man takes news philosophically, whereas a city man is likely to hear it with panic.

Yet, as I noted, for those of us who live near or in the city, absorbing a country psychology usually doesn't mean going off to a lightly populated, out-of-the-way place—although, it is fine to do this if you can and wish to do so. Instead, with a slightly different focus, it means appreciating where we already live *but in a richer way*. With a sense of the simple themes such as those lightly touched upon in this book, an attitude can change and with it a perspective. The following words of a New Yorker who read sections of an earlier draft of this book reflect the outlook I had hoped for in writing it—no matter under what geographical conditions one lives.

When I have the correct perspective I find that there is a lovely, spare asceticism about the city—especially

New York City—from the architecture to the minimalism imposed by the sheer lack of horizontal space. With the correct outlook, I can make life in the city like that of the fourth-century desert *abbas* (fathers) and *ammas* (mothers) of Syria and northern Egypt who lived in sparsely populated areas.

As you point out, with the lessons of gratitude, simplicity, mindfulness, compassion and your other themes before me, I don't experience the city as a jumble, as many people do. Instead, I can appreciate the bubble of silence that every New Yorker usually allows other New Yorkers to feel by not being intrusive or immediately open and friendly. I find it gives one time to make a thoughtful decision about responses or overtures, and whether or not one will choose to make them.

With the right "eyes" what appears to be speed and uncontrolled hubbub is really energy if you accept that the surface is active and moving but underneath there is purposeful depth that supports life—like an ocean. It stimulates me. I find I have painful withdrawal symptoms without it.

The complexity of the people and act of living in the city is like this gigantic jigsaw puzzle that is meant for each of us to solve. When one finds a piece that fits with another piece it gives the greatest contentment. Sometimes in a whole day, a whole section of the giant picture that's hidden in the puzzle becomes absolutely clear to me. And I guess I think I find these pieces by trying to practice, as you suggest in your book, such essential things as kindness, gentleness, and letting go.

Given this sentiment, we can see that, with a bit of attention, living the themes of a simple, reflective, generous life can be accomplished anywhere. Whenever I am tempted to become wistful about my time as a youth on the farm or the intense life I live now, I stop myself and recognize that I can change what is preventing me from being mindful and reflective with just a bit of effort, no matter where I live. With a country psychology I can even be content in spite of or *because* of living in or near a city. I just need to appreciate and incorporate the right perspective and priorities that lead to compassion and contentment.

I used to feel it was good when I prioritized my schedule, and I suspect it is necessary when things are busy and seem out of whack. But I also remember Stephen Covey's suggestion that an even more important step than prioritizing your schedule is scheduling your priorities. We have more power to do this than we think.

Robert Fulghum, author of *All I Really Need to Know I Learned in Kindergarten*, tells a story of a man who complained daily about the lunch he brought to work. Finally, when this had gone on for weeks, one of his coworkers got up the courage to ask who made his sandwiches anyway. To which the man responded, "Why, I do."

We are responsible for our own lives. Just as I unconsciously did as a youngster on the farm, I must consciously:

- Slow down by taking a few breaths as I walk somewhere or am about to answer the phone or sit down at the computer.

- See the day before me—people, things, myself—as they are, not as I want them to be.
- Take a walk, not "take a think," and be open to all the gifts around me—whether it be a forest I feel is detoxifying me or the bustle of a city where I feel the impulse to smile at the energy around me.
- Appreciate the wonders of who I am and all the people, benefits, and inspiring challenges around me that won't be there forever.
- Allow myself a few moments each day in silence and solitude, in my own mental forest with a stream in it, where I can simply breathe, relax, and be, and can know in my heart that I have enough for now to be at peace . . . yes, to know I have *enough*, I am *enough*.

When you relax, breathe deeply, and are mindful, meditative, and alive with a sense of inner ease, this state is not only a source of personal contentment (although it is certainly that); your mere quiet, reassuring presence can be a gift encouraging serenity in others as well.

twelve

MIND YOUR OWN NEGATIVE
PREDICTIONS *and* EVALUATIONS

For me, North Carolina represents the best of both the North and the South. I just love the Tar Heel State. It has sophisticated university cities, the ocean, the mountains, and all the rural area you would want in between. My trip to speak to sheriffs on applied psychology for law enforcement officers was to the "in between" area.

As I launched into my first presentation, I was as animated as ever. I have never learned to pace myself as some of my colleagues do who can seem to wipe off their desk, sit down on it, and then lecture for hours. I find myself moving around the room, telling stories, and trying to relate principles that are practical and easy to remember.

When I present, chemistry hopefully develops between me and the audience. In this case, that is just what happened . . . for the *most* part. While most of the men present—at the time all sheriffs in this area were male—were laughing, there was one who through every story, no matter how rollicking it might be for the rest of the class, just sat there with a stone face. Normally this is to be expected, and it is no big deal. However, for some reason, this morning it was really getting to me, so the negative dialogue started to build within me.

"I don't have to put up with this. Here I am giving my all, and he doesn't even appreciate it. How resistant can you be? He should be up here in my place. Then he would see!" It finally got so crazy that I thought, "Well, I don't have to put up with this. After the break, I'll just give the material straight out rather than putting on such a show."

Well, the break did come, and the fellow I had the inner dialogue about stood up straight and walked right toward me. He looked down at me (he was huge) and said, "I don't think you should be a teacher," and then paused. (At that moment I thought, "Didn't I have this guy pegged correctly? Am I not a great diagnostician?") He finally broke into a youthful grin and said, "You should be an actor. That was terrific!" And being the ethical guy that I am, I replied, "You know, I knew from the look on your face that you were really enjoying it."

We predict what people are thinking and make assessments often in a negative direction without really knowing what is going on. Is it any wonder then that we are surprised and caught up short when the opposite or something other than what we expected jumps out at us?

A priest who teaches at Georgetown University told me that he was walking to school one day and encountered a homeless man asking for money. The priest decided to give him some change he had in his pocket. When he did, the man thanked him and said "Please pray for me." The priest nodded, said he would, and then

Things are not as they seem.

added almost as a matter of course as he was turning away, "Please pray for me too." At which point, the man said in return, "Why? What seems to be the problem?"

He hadn't expected this and started to mumble some response. At which point, the man took his hands, looked up at the heavens, and prayed out loud for him for a few seconds, then let go of his hands and wished him well. Later, the priest told me he was so surprised at this because he had prejudged the man and the situation. The encounter opened his eyes and his heart to seeing things without preconceptions.

Being open and seeking *not* to be judgmental are often quite elusive undertakings, no matter how aware we try to be. Even when we think we have a sense of openness and are sensitive to what is happening around us, often we are not. We can't be, because we never have all the information. This is illustrated well by Stephen Covey:

> One Sunday morning I was on a subway in New York. People were sitting quietly—some reading newspapers, some lost in thought, some resting with their eyes closed. It was a calm and peaceful scene.
>
> Then suddenly, a man and his children entered the subway car. The children were so loud and rambunctious that instantly the whole climate changed.

The man sat down next to me and closed his eyes, apparently oblivious to the situation. The children were yelling back and forth, throwing things, even grabbing people's papers. It was very disturbing. And yet, the man sitting next to me did nothing.

It was difficult not to feel irritated. I could not believe that he could be so insensitive as to let his children run wild like that and do nothing about it, taking no responsibility at all. It was easy to see that everyone else on the subway felt irritated too. So, finally, with what I felt was unusual patience and restraint, I turned to him and said, "Sir, your children are really disturbing a lot of people. I wonder if you wouldn't control them a little more?"

The man lifted his gaze as if to come to a consciousness of the situation for the first time and said softly, "Oh, you're right, I guess I should do something about it. We just came from the hospital where their mother died about an hour ago. I don't know what to think, and I guess they don't know how to handle it differently."

Can you imagine what I felt at that moment? My paradigm shifted. Suddenly I *saw* differently, I *thought* differently, I *behaved* differently. My irritation vanished. I didn't have to worry about controlling my attitude or my behavior; my heart was filled with the man's pain. Feelings of sympathy and compassion flowed freely. "Your wife just died? Oh, I'm so sorry! Can you tell me about it? What can I do to help?" Everything changed in an instant.

People are often concerned about the negative impact of their ignorance. They feel it is what they don't know that will hurt them, and this of course is true, to a certain extent. However I believe that an even more subtle, insidious danger than ignorance is that which we think we already know but actually don't. True sensitivity and real wisdom begin with recognizing this fact by minding our predictions or evaluations.

At times we tend to be so hardhearted that even when presented with contrary information, we "dig in our heels" and hold onto our opinions rather than being open enough to let in new information that may prove us wrong. I think the following story shared by Anthony de Mello illustrates this point well.

A woman suddenly stops a man walking down the street and says, "Henry, I am so happy to see you after all these years! My, how you have changed. I remember you as being tall, and you seem so much shorter now. You used to have a pale complexion, and it is really so ruddy now. Good grief, how you have changed in five years!"

Finally, the man gets a chance to interject, "But my name isn't Henry!"

To which the persistent woman calmly responds, "Oh, so you changed your name too!"

Recognizing that what you perceive is never *the total truth allows you to remain open, flexible, a continual learner in life, and prepares the inner soil well for the planting and growth of new wisdom that is the lifeblood of contentment in the now.*

thirteen

MINE THE CRITICISMS YOU RECEIVE *from* OTHERS, *but* DON'T GET CARRIED AWAY!

A dear friend of mine used to share the following saying about criticism when the time called for it: "The first time someone calls you a horse's rear end, take offense. If a second person calls you a horse's rear end about the same thing, think it over. However, if a third person calls you a horse's rear end, again about the same thing, *buy a saddle!*"

For most of us, criticism is difficult to accept. It is easy to be a prophet to others, but not to ourselves. One instance of this still comes to my mind even though it happened many, many years ago.

I opened a letter from a very famous churchman in the United States. He was doing wonderful work. However, when I read his note to me, I became furious. I thought to myself, "You are doing very good work, but how you plan to go about it is slick." Now, as you know, when you become really angry at someone there are two rules to follow: keep your mouth shut, and stay away from the phone. So, naturally, I called him.

After I shared with him what I felt, he said we should sit down and chat about it. When we did, the conversation went nowhere. I would give him an illustration, and he would have an excuse. I'd give him another illustration, and he would have another excuse. Finally, I realized this was ridiculous. I was focusing on the lyrics of his behavior (what he had done), and it was the music of his actions (how he did it) that was really important. I could also see that in trying to present my concerns I had truly messed up the whole encounter. I had hurt him and caused him what we call in my business "narcissistic injury." When that happens, little if anything can be accomplished, because you have insulted who the person is rather than focused on his behavior.

As a result, I tried to back out of the encounter with as much grace as I could muster. Then, as I was doing this, he said to me, "You know that when you called and said these things about me, I called up several persons and asked them about *you*." As he related to me what he had heard, I realized that I wasn't being called to be prophet to him, he was being called to be prophet to me. I also came to appreciate something that I don't like to admit, but which I believe is true: namely, no matter how poor the motivations of the person who says negative things about you are, what he or she says is true to some extent. If you are able to mine these truths you will truly deepen your self-awareness and be freer to learn in the future. I certainly can attest to this reality in my own life.

Once when I fell into the basement of my psyche because of a series of negative events in my life, I thought to myself, "Well, as long as I am down here, I might as well look around." What I came to grips with were some of my defenses, fears, and shames. I saw how I had been cowardly and greedy and had let down those I had recently met along with those I had known for years. The insights were not pretty, but they helped prune me down to size, my real size. There is little to fear when you are simply who you are—nothing more, nothing less.

Living fully requires us to be open to criticism from others. When we close ourselves down we can miss so much helpful information. Unfortunately, when faced with the challenge to do this, because of our fears of failure and criticism we often hold back, defend ourselves, or tell people that they just don't understand. We also spend too much time worrying about what people will think. Instead, we need to put such undue concerns into their proper place so we don't get carried away by the criticisms we receive.

Turn present darkness into new light for the future.

In *The Te of Piglet*, Benjamin Hoff helps us put criticism and the people who offer it in perspective. I dearly love the following story and reflect on it when I get upset over what someone has said to me.

> While traveling separately through the countryside one late afternoon, a Hindu, a Rabbi, and a Critic were caught by a terrific thunderstorm. They sought shelter at the same nearby farmhouse.

"That storm will be raging for hours," the farmer told them. "You'd better stay here for the night. The problem is, there's only room enough for two of you. One of you'll have to sleep in the barn."

"I'll be the one," said the Hindu. "A little hardship is nothing to me." He went out to the barn.

A few minutes later there was a knock on the door. It was the Hindu. "I'm sorry," he told the others, "but there is a cow in the barn. According to my religion, cows are sacred, and one must not intrude into their space."

"Don't worry," said the Rabbi. "Make yourself comfortable here. I'll go sleep in the barn." He went out to the barn.

A few minutes later, there was a knock at the door. It was the Rabbi. "I hate to be a bother," he said, "but there is a pig in the barn. I wouldn't feel comfortable sharing my sleeping quarters with a pig."

"Oh, all right," said the Critic. "I'll go sleep in the barn." He went out to the barn.

A few minutes later, there was a knock at the door. It was the cow and the pig.

Remember this, and you will both mine the criticisms you receive and not become overwhelmed by persons who seem to go around seeing the shortcomings in others (especially you!) with acuity, while failing to ever look at themselves in a fashion that is both kind and clear. If they did look at themselves with clarity, then the way they criticize people wouldn't be so destructive.

When people chat with me about receiving criticism, they often also broach the topic of giving criticism. When this happens, my response usually is twofold: first, don't criticize others; just present the concern you have in summary form, and let the summary call them to look differently at what they are doing in life. And second, if possible, help people change by creatively having them see the consequences of their behavior.

The best example I have heard of this was in a story from a private school in Washington, DC. It seems they were faced with a difficulty that can arise when children pass on to a new stage in their social development.

A number of twelve-year-old girls were beginning to use lipstick for the first time. The problem that developed was that, after they would put it on in the bathroom, which was fine, they would then press their lips to the mirror leaving dozens of little lip prints. This would leave an extra chore for the maintenance crew who came in at night to clean the building. When this happened once, nothing was done. However, when it became a daily ritual for the girls, the principal realized something had to be done.

She called the girls into the bathroom and met them there with the maintenance man. She explained to them that she knew they were doing it for fun, but there were consequences that possibly they didn't know about. She then went on to explain that the custodian had to clean the mirrors every night, and this took unnecessary time and energy on his part.

She noted that they were showing obvious disdain for what she was saying, and some even yawned and smirked at one another.

Without reacting to them, she went on by saying that possibly they didn't realize how much effort was required, so she wanted them to see what was involved so they could better understand, and she nodded to the maintenance man.

Whereupon he took out a long-handled squeegee, dipped it into the toilet, and cleaned the mirror with it. After this, there were no lip prints on the mirrors.

As the person who told me the story aptly noted, "There are teachers . . . and then there are *educators*." When we creatively and humbly receive and offer others criticism in an inoffensive manner, the chance of impact will obviously be better.

Contentment grows when you can see everyone as your teacher. Then you will learn much about yourself and feel greater peace. You will be less defensive when you get feedback you don't like or feel might be wrong.

———————

fourteen

MAKE NEW FRIENDS
with FAILURE

No one likes to fail. Some people truly get rattled by even the possibility of failure and shrink back from any serious involvement. This is a shame since their talents don't get fully developed and, just as sad, the rest of us are deprived of experiencing their gifts to the fullest.

Once when I presented a lecture on being a compassionate presence in the world, one person said to me, "You make being helpful sound so positive, but I have this fearful question nagging me: What if I fail?"

I responded, "Well, let me assure you then. Often you *will*."

At this, the questioner, with eyes wide open, made a face and said, "Oh, great! Thanks!" and then the whole audience laughed, including the two of us.

The reality, though, is that the attempt to live a life of contentment brings with it a certain amount of failure, and the part of this failure that hurts the most is the recognition of the personal limits, poor motivations, and personal inadequacies we have hidden from ourselves. The problem with intimacy with people in pain is that, while we try to help them trust and open themselves to their own inadequacies and faults, we are called to see our own blemishes as well.

Concrete love also calls us, as persons seeking to be helpful, to ask the right question in relationships. How often we ask, "Would you like to have what *I* want to give you now?" when the real question of love is, "What is it that *you* want, need, and are able to handle now?"

That second question is much more difficult because the answer is unpredictable. We may be inconvenienced or made temporarily uncomfortable when we try to fulfill the request. We may have to sit with people experiencing the darkness in ways that make us feel uncomfortable because the questions they ask have no answers. After all, there is no answer to why suffering happens in a supposedly good world. From what I have noted thus far, it is obvious that helping other people requires humility and a willingness to fail. Otherwise, our sense of contentment with ourselves, with others, and in the interactions we have with them will be unnecessarily disturbed.

One way to strengthen our ability to be a compassionate presence to others is to more readily appreciate ourselves and to recognize our own foibles, even to the point where we can gently laugh at ourselves. When people enjoy themselves and can get in touch with their own beauty, they can even reach the point of teasing themselves. This frees them up to be more open to others instead of being overly protective due to concern about their own ego. When this happens they can enjoy their recognition of their foibles through a sense of humor about themselves. Thus, in turn, they will feel freer and more at peace in their interactions, even with strangers.

In my travels I have seen this gift exemplified by many groups, but none as much as the rural Newfoundlanders who reside in the easternmost part of Canada. They are truly people of simplicity and joy, and to be with them is wonderful. Yet they are often teased by people from other Canadian provinces about their simplicity. In response, they do not seek to deny it or to be pseudo-sophisticated about it. Instead, they impishly tease both themselves and those whom they are with so that when you are with them you can't help but have fun yourself.

I have been to Newfoundland many times, but my mind goes back to the first time I was there to offer some lectures. I had completed the lectures and was sitting on an Air Canada jet getting ready to take off for Halifax and then proceed to Boston. I am basically a no-nonsense traveler; I am there to fly, not to bond with the person sitting next to me, so I was thanking God that the seat next to me was empty. Now, I am going to share an important theological fact: never thank God for something until you have that gift firmly in hand! Because just as I was smiling at my good fortune, a person plopped into the seat next to me. I thought to myself, "Oh, no, a plopper." I put my book up in front of my face to indicate my desire for privacy.

This tactic was to no avail, because a few moments later a hand came to the top of the book and pulled it down, and a round ruddy face looked me straight in the eye and asked, "Are you from Newfoundland? Are you a Newfee?" Surprised, I said in return, "No. I'm not from Newfoundland. I'm not a Newfee." To which he said proudly, while patting his chest, "I'm a Newfee!" I thought to myself in my usual dry way, "Well, I am happy for you and the children."

He then suddenly asked, "Do you know where the Newfees keep their armies?" Now totally puzzled by the question and the encounter, I said, "No." He gleefully replied, "Up their sleevies!" He finally had me, so I said while laughing in spite of myself, "Are we going to do this the whole way to Halifax?" at which point someone from the French part of the island took down a fiddle from the overhead bin and started playing. Do you want to hear the worst part? I started to sing along with all of them!

Making mistakes (lots of them!) is natural if you are fully involved in life.

What a flight it was! What wonderful people Newfoundlanders are. I love them. Their joy and ability to poke fun at their own sense of simplicity helps others around them see how uptight they themselves are, and to relax and accept their own ordinariness in the process as well. You begin to see that true ordinariness is tangible goodness.

It's wonderful when we can indeed laugh at ourselves, our dark sides, and our foibles. Without this quality, we have a tendency to bury our negative style through denial or bravado. When we do, we decrease our own sensitivity to self (self-awareness/appreciation) and, in turn, increase our defensiveness with others.

A compassionate presence, true self-awareness, and a sense of humor all go well together. They set the stage for us to relax enough to see ourselves honestly, to take ourselves less seriously, and to learn how we can best be a healing presence to others without unduly carrying the burden of our pride in the process. Being at ease with ourselves is a great and gentle gift; without it, presence to others becomes just another chore rather than a wonder to experience even in the darkest of times.

The reality is that much of what we find dark and difficult is unfortunately partly of our own doing. Yoda, the wisdom figure and Jedi Master in the movie *The Empire Strikes Back*, makes this point. In one scene, Yoda urges Luke Skywalker, the young disciple who came to him for mentoring, to enter a cave that seems to emanate danger and fear. When Luke asks Yoda, "What's in the cave?" his simple reply is, "Only what you bring in with you."

The same can be said of us as we enter "the cave" of reaching out to others and feel our ego is on the line. As in times of silence, solitude, and quiet meditation, many things from myriad sources may tear at us. But chief among them are our interior demons and fear of failure—as if when we make a mistake, we are a total failure. It is good for us to be aware of our interior darkness, defensiveness, and the sources of what makes failure and other difficult experiences in life worse for us. For many of us these sources include such things as:

- Lack of self-awareness, self-acceptance, and self-love
- Dishonesty

- Intolerance of others
- Unfinished business with family, friends, and coworkers
- Suppressed or repressed negative feelings
- Poorly developed ethics, beliefs, and values
- Attachments or addictions
- Hidden, past, or unintegrated embarrassments
- Resistance to intimacy or change
- Failure to take care of ourselves
- Lack of honesty and openness with others or ourselves in meditation
- Lack of meaning in life
- Ungrieved losses
- Greed
- Unreasonable expectations of self and others
- A sense of entitlement
- Undealt-with anger
- Unwillingness to risk and an inordinate need for security
- Inability to experience quiet in our lives
- Unhealthy self-involvement or, at the other extreme, lack of healthy self-interest
- Failure to set priorities in our own lives
- Irresponsibility
- Being too much of a perfectionist or inordinately self-critical
- Unwillingness to accept love except in ways we have predetermined as meaningful
- Fear of responsibility and a tendency to project blame

A true encounter with self can be like a psychological or spiritual mirror. It crisply reflects those partially hidden and disguised parts of our personality that keep us chained to a philosophy of living which isn't open or mature enough. The mirror reflects our own sometimes rigid defenses, personal immaturities, unresolved, repressed issues, hidden motivations, tenacious defenses, erroneous (yet comfortable) self-definitions, and chameleon-like behaviors. In essence, it confronts us with the darkness of our own unintegrated self. And isn't that great?

Yes, failure and interactions that open us up to our limits and denials give us information that can help us to transform our lives in a positive way. I have long felt that when I get upset at people, these very people are my spiritual directors because they call me to shape my life in a new way, facing both my darkness and my talents with a more complete, and thus healthier, sense of self. This can then lead to a more responsible, honest style of relating. Once again, anything negative said about or to us, no matter how poor the motivation of the person saying it, is true to some extent. If we mine these truths we can be freer. This is a gift that success can never offer us in quite the same way.

Failure and other negative experiences are not what really disturbs your sense of well-being. Rather it is your view of not succeeding or your perception that an outcome is terrible that disturbs you. Change your perspective and the upset will lessen, leaving you with new knowledge and inner freedom.

fifteen

Appreciate *the* Real Meaning *and* Power *of* Your Own "Self-Whispers"

One of the nicest settings that I ever had for my clinical practice was in Marriottsville, Maryland. My office was in a spirituality center surrounded by 128 acres of fields and woodlands. Once, a peahen took up residence outside my window. Another time, for several days, a fawn lay under my window.

Given the presence of majestic oaks and mature spruces, the center was especially breathtaking in the snow. So the first snowstorm of the season was quite an event to celebrate, and one winter it chose to come when I was there to see patients. I looked up and absorbed the beauty as it coated the landscape; I smiled and thought, "Wow."

Immediately following that experience, I got caught up in the back-to-back sessions of the day and looked out again when it was early afternoon, and the snow had started to really mount up. When I saw it all, the previous poetic appreciation of the landscape immediately disappeared. Now I thought, "Oh, no! How am I ever going to get out of here when the day is over?" (Obviously my spiritual appreciation of nature is not too consistent.)

Just as I was thinking this, the phone rang, and it was a patient who was also a psychologist. She said, "I am not coming in today." Still annoyed about the weather, I said, "Well, it is up to you." She could hear something in the tone of my voice and said, "Well, you are not going to charge me for the missed session are you?" I replied, a bit irked by the question, "Well, you know you need to give twenty-four hours notice if you don't wish to be charged."

You could tell by the intake in her voice that she was shocked and annoyed as she responded, "Well, then, *I'm* coming!" and she abruptly hung up before I could say anything. As I sat there I thought, "Oh, no. Under the circumstances, I would now willingly pay her *not* to come in."

When she finally arrived, she surprised me. Rather than displaying anger, she showed something totally different. She was smiling. After taking it in, I asked, "How come you are smiling? I thought you would be furious at me for the way I responded over the phone."

She continued smiling and replied quite simply, "*You* were angry." To which I replied, "No I wasn't."

She looked at me puzzled and said, "You weren't?"

"No, I was *furious*. You caught me when I was in a real mood about the weather. But I still don't know why you are smiling rather than angry."

"Well, when you were angry at me, I experienced the *real* you."

After a pause that allowed me to take in what she was saying, I saw this as a chance to use the situation to her advantage. I pointed out a disparity that was important for her to recognize about her own self-image and said, "It seems to me that in the

> *Know the reputation you have with yourself.*

past when I have given you positive feedback, this didn't seem like the real me. However, when I behaved poorly and reacted in a negative way, for some reason this seemed more real to you. Why do you think you hear positive feedback in a whisper and negative reactions as thunder?"

It is important for us to have an accurate self-image. If we do, we can be freer and more integrated and, in turn, be compassionate to many different types of people, no matter how they react to us. This will save psychic energy instead of wasting it on trying to develop several personalities or masks depending upon whom we are with. It will help us to develop as persons.

In addition, it will help us better monitor the meaning or messages we give ourselves all day. This is referred to in psychology as "self-talk" or what I prefer to call "self-whispers," since they often go unrecognized and therefore unexamined or unchallenged. With a real sense of self we can approach situations with a greater sense of certainty and humility. Consequently, rather than feeling we need to always seek approval or reinforcement (though some is natural and good), we can act out of our true identity. If positive results occur, fine; if negative ones occur, well, fine too, because they will teach us something.

When we feel ourselves becoming anxious, depressed, or stressed, we can ask questions that will get us back in touch with our true calling (mentioned in the beginning of this book). This will help us to see that our fears and "dis-ease" are arising out of playing a role, fearing rejection, or being revealed as a charlatan of some type. To help us counter this, some questions we need to ask ourselves when having negative feelings include:

- Why am I making myself so angry in this situation?
- What is it about this situation that is making me so uncomfortable?
- What do I fear losing in this situation?
- What am I demanding of the people around me, and why is it so upsetting that I am not getting it?
- What is the worst thing that could happen if I said or did _____?
- Why am I so worried about the possibility of people seeing me as imperfect, unhelpful, a failure, not unique, self-seeking, self-protecting, greedy, addicted, or ignorant? In some cases isn't this certainly true?
- What is the reason I am giving people the power to upset me?
- What is the most helpful thing I can do in this instance to learn about myself and the people and situation at hand?
- If I am alone, what is it that I am concentrating on in myself that is transforming solitude into loneliness and self-deprecation?
- Why am I taking a possibly annoying event and making it into something worse?

All the above basic questions, which we often don't stop to ask ourselves, can help free us from wasteful ways of thinking. We can be more content with ourselves as we travel our psychological and spiritual journeys in life. These questions are designed to break the logjam of unrealistic expectations, unnecessary fears, crippling angers, destructive anxieties, and undue distress. Then it becomes possible to live with greater clarity, contentment, and compassion. The questions also produce a good deal of information on how we are falling into patterns of pleasing, grasping, and controlling rather than living out of our central identity ("name") and simply flowing with our lives.

The freedom to live this way has a price though. The price is honesty and humility. Without these, we are not clear about what is before us, we fail to be content, and we often lack the purity of motivations to help us be really compassionate without wanting anything in return. Yes, there is a cost, but the serenity that results is truly worth the effort.

If you are aware that you have been given myriad talents (some not yet explored), as an act of gratitude seek to enhance and share them as best as you can. Never, never forget they are in fact gifts, *and you will be content to be who you are—which will also be a gift to others.*

II.

—

Five Minutes *a* Day: Spending Thirty Days *"in the* Country" *on* Retreat

ENTERING YOUR OWN FRESH STREAMS *of* CONTENTMENT

No one gets up in the morning with the commitment, "Today I shall fool myself, be discontented, and not be compassionate to those in my life." Yet, if we are honest with ourselves, we must admit that, more often than we'd like, we behave as if we had made just such a crazy commitment. Such admissions make it hard not to get discouraged and say, "Life is like that, and this is just the way I am."

To some extent this is true. At times life is brimming with injustices, tragedies, and confusion. Contentment is so elusive and real compassion seems impossible given all that is on our shoulders. The bottom line is life isn't easy.

Still, while life is not easy, it is also true that there are some simple truths that can help us to live more richly, no matter who we are or what our circumstances are. More to the point of this small book, life can be filled with greater clarity, compassion, and *contentment*. Yes. It's possible but not easy—patience, persistence, and a desire for a healthier perspective are all needed. Moreover, these qualities must be brought to mind every day if we are to be able to both enjoy and share the fruits of such wonderful, renewing streams of serenity.

Given this, to make the most of the core of this book and build on it, I offer a number of essential themes to serve as a basis for a month of reflections on aspects of the ideas of clarity, contentment, and compassion. By calling it "Spending Thirty Days 'in the Country' on Retreat," I am obviously not in any way suggesting that you run away from your life to a rural setting. What I am encouraging, though, is that the comments offered function best when:

- Reflected on early in the day when you have a quiet moment by yourself
- Recalled several times during the day to see how they apply realistically and practically to your feelings, thoughts, beliefs, and actions
- Reviewed once again before going to bed

The nice thing about following this approach is that in just a few minutes each day, many of the basic themes of clarity, contentment, compassion, and other relevant points raised in your own mind will have an opportunity to take root and bear fruit.

Some of the points may not turn out to be meaningful for you. Others may be only of short-term value. Some, hopefully, will prove of lasting use. However, by approaching the material in this way, you will have given the overall themes of clarity, contentment, and compassion a higher profile in your outlook on life. You may be surprised by the results.

The final step, after having finished a month of scattered reflections, is to take some final minutes to see what overall psychological or spiritual theme you have discovered to help you lead a life that is rich and full. In other words, what one or two sentences seem to sum up the lessons of clarity, contentment, and compassion that you have learned? What one phrase might help you to easily recall what is truly important in how you lead your life and might quickly bring to mind a healthy attitude for approaching life—especially in difficult or confusing circumstances?

You may ask, quite candidly, what motivation you could possibly have for doing this, given your very busy schedule. Although it may seem unrealistic to say this, I believe it can transform the tone of how you live the rest of your life and positively impact others. Certainly, if this is a possibility, it is worth a try. And so this section may be the most important part of the book for you *if* it is taken to heart. I repeat once again the words of William James:

> Sow an action, and you reap a habit;
> Sow a habit, and you reap a character;
> Sow a character, and you reap a destiny.

Day 1

EXPERIENCE *the* POSITIVE PARADOX *of* BEING GRATEFUL

A wonderful friend of mine told me that he recently spent time with a person who was in the mid-phase of Alzheimer's disease. He described how he would sit with him and help fill in the blanks that had been forgotten; this gave the person great joy. After he told me this, he paused for a moment and finally added, "I was privileged to be his memory. I hope that if the same befalls me, someone will be there to be mine."

At the time, I thought, "How right you are," and nodded agreement. Yet after a few weeks had passed, I considered what it would be like for me to experience *spiritual* Alzheimer's, where I lost memory for many of the little things people had done for me in life.

Many of us tend to think the good things that have happened were because of our efforts—and to some degree this is true. However, we were given genetic gifts that weren't the result of our efforts. There are also so many ways that friends, family, coworkers, and even new acquaintances have helped us achieve what we have. No matter how talented we are and how hard we strive, we never reach our goals on our own. Forgetting that is a fatal blow to being a continually grateful person.

A Simple Practice

Recall the faces of those who encouraged, teased, challenged, and inspired you. Take some time with these people and events in your mind and say softly, "Thank you. Thank you. Thank you." The positive paradox is that to the grateful, more is given (or at least noticed and enjoyed).

Day 2

What *if* We Gave
Someone *a* Real Gift?

I once had a colleague who was very small in stature. He was so short, in fact, it seemed it would be quicker to jump over him than to go around him. However, he was very big in heart. His generous nature always made me stop to reflect on how conditional my sharing with people is. After reflecting more deeply on this, I realized that most of what we give to others is conditional. If we smile, we expect warmth in return. If we give advice, we expect people to both appreciate and follow it. When this doesn't happen, we feel used and unappreciated which leads to negative emotions such as feeling resentful or foolish. This leaves us with a small, yet significant, question: "What if we gave to people and expected absolutely nothing in return?"

A Simple Practice

Today, offer a space for someone without any expectations for anything in return. Share a smile or encouraging comment, leave a larger gratuity at a hotel where you are staying on the morning of your departure, respond to a request without seeing it as doing something for others; in other words, give expecting nothing in return and see how freeing this is to both you and the person receiving it.

Day 3

LET EXPERIENCES *be* BEACONS—
not MERELY SOUVENIRS

During a break in a lecture I was giving in Edinburgh, Scotland, I shared with one of the persons in the audience that I would be leaving right after my presentation to spend a few days on the Isle of Iona. In response, she smiled, looked off in the distance as if she were envisioning her last magical, mystical trip there, and said, "Ah, it is certainly a sacred spot." Then she turned to me and said, "If you can, put it in your suitcase and take it home with you."

At the time, I remember laughing with her at this comment. Yet later, after my visit, I realized what she really intended. By her comment I knew that I would be foolish if I truly didn't take steps to bring the experience of Iona with me.

We have a choice with grace-filled memories: we can put them on a shelf to recall as nice dead things from the past, or we can put them in our hearts and take them home so they can become beacons to shine new perspectives on the rest of our life. If the Isle of Iona—with its spiritual aura and history—could not teach me to live with greater sensitivity, then how little the experience truly meant.

A Simple Practice

Seek to recall poignant or unique moments in your life—long past or recent—and see what such experiences might mean for how you live your life today. For instance, I recall the times in my life that persons have behaved in ways that really inspired me. How might I follow their examples today? There have also been moments of quiet for me—on the west coast of Ireland, by a lake in Pasadena, in Newfoundland, and in a hospital chapel in New York City—when I felt centered and appreciative of the need for some silence. Might I imagine myself in those places for a few minutes each day to quiet myself down so I don't compulsively run to my grave instead? Now, turn to your own life: How might you use your reflective imagination to do the same with memories of moments with people and experiences that could enable you to live your life in a richer, more serene, and more compassionate way?

Day 4

SHORTEN *your* ANNOYANCES

Someone who always seemed annoyed was described to me like this: "He is a very balanced person. He has a chip on *both* his shoulders."

We may not be this bad, but all of us are sometimes guilty of foolishly making our annoyances last longer than necessary. When something happens to us that we don't like, we often let it fester. If someone dares to ask us, "Why are you holding onto the negative?" we might get even more annoyed and say, "Well, wouldn't you be annoyed by this?" The sense is that it is natural to get annoyed and stay that way.

While this might be the attitude of many people to-day, do we need to make prolonging annoyance part of *our* natural mode of operating? On a visit to Florida, I was staying at hotel that had a travel desk that confirmed your reservation and even printed out boarding passes. I went to the desk just after 1:00 p.m. What I didn't realize is that it closed at 1:00 p.m., so they couldn't help me. I became annoyed. Now, while it makes sense that I didn't like being inconvenienced, it made absolutely no sense for me to stay annoyed longer than a moment. If someone poked you with a stick, would you then take that stick and poke yourself continually for the next half hour? And when questioned about it, would you defend your silly behavior by saying, "It's natural, *everyone* does it."

A Simple Practice

The next time something negative happens that annoys you—someone jumps in line ahead of you or cuts you off on the road—and you get upset initially, take a few breaths and ask yourself why you keep poking yourself with a stick by staying annoyed.

Day 5

EXPERIENCE MINDFUL JOY
more OFTEN

The philosopher Søren Kierkegaard once said: "Most people pursue pleasure with such breathless haste that they hurry past it." This mindless type of living is often seen as both necessary and practical in modern society. But, in truth, is it?

I find that people I admire have a great deal on their plate. However, they face what is in front of them with true attention. As a matter of fact, because they are really listening instead of merely hearing others while waiting for their opportunity to speak, they tend to more quickly grasp a situation. Like a doctor who has a full waiting room but knows she can only see one patient at a time, they are little distracted with what is coming next.

We spend so little time on planning (a true mindful activity) and so much on preoccupation that we enjoy little of our life. For instance, are you enjoying the words you are reading on this page and reflecting on how you might apply them to your own life to make it more meaningful and fun, or are you rushing along trying to get to the next practice or next suggestion on living a more serene life? Being mindful allows you to enjoy fully the meal (experience) in front of you. Being mindless has you at best enjoying the menu but never experiencing the meal fully. It is like having photographs of a place you have visited but were never fully present to because you were so intent on capturing the scene that you never took the time to enjoy it.

A Simple Practice

When you get up in the morning, take a few breaths before you get out of bed. Listen to the sounds around you, and be grateful for your life. Tell yourself that you will enter the day with low expectations or demands for what you want, but that you will have high hopes for what you will see and experience when you pay attention. Catch yourself when you are rushing through breakfast; instead, enjoy the taste of the coffee or tea, the crunch of your cereal, or the sweetness or texture of a cereal bar. Which would you rather experience: slowly enjoying a frankfurter or vegetable wrap, or swallowing chunks of steak, fish, or chicken without even tasting them? Remember: it is not whether you learn to be mindful always and forever that is important; it is reminding yourself to be mindful *now*.

Day 6

To Clarity, *add* Contentment

One goal of clarity is to save us from wasting or misdirecting energy; contentment results from knowing what to do with that energy once it is saved. When we look out the window in the morning and see what is—not what we wish would be—and embrace it, it is the beginning of an attitude of contentment. When we drop defenses or addictions and become like children learning to play, then we do not feel what we may experience as boredom or lack of direction. Rather we begin to set the stage for contentment. Contentment is not merely being satisfied with what you have, although many people believe and settle for this definition and direction to their lives. It is more than that: it is having an attitude capable of embracing fully both what is and what comes our way.

A Simple Practice

Catch yourself when you are comparing what you have or what is coming your way with what you like best or feel you deserve. Instead, seek to look at everything with a sense of intrigue and see what comes of it. When waiting in line, don't simply seek to move quickly through it but allow yourself to experience the wait in a new way, devoid of expectation. Who knows—you may find it a time to settle down, breathe, be mindful, relax, and see!

Day 7

SEARCH *for* SPECIFIC TRUTHS (THEY ARE HARDER *to* FACE *but* MUCH MORE HELPFUL)

The search for "the truth" doesn't amount to or change much. However, being open to specific truths about yourself and how your perception of something is not totally correct can be very instructive. Yet, often we don't want to be enlightened in this way. When my wife tells me things that I don't like to hear, I often remark, "I don't have to sit here and listen to these truths!" However, these little upsets at seeing something about my behavior, attitude, or style of thinking can lead to real knowledge. To embrace this knowledge might take a bit of humility, but the reward is wonderful. When we take knowledge and add humility, we get wisdom. When we add this wisdom to compassion, we get love. And that is quite a reward!

A Simple Practice

Personal darkness is not simply an encounter with what we don't like, although surely it is that as well. It is also an invitation to sacrifice one level of experience for another.

The next time you hear something upsetting about yourself, your behavior, or your attitude, instead of defending yourself or reacting, reflect: What in this encounter is really bothering me? How can I understand this better? How can I examine my motivations and see if they are as pure as I'd like? What is behind my anxieties and anger around this topic? How can I mine this wonderful information without dismissing it by projecting the blame on another, beating myself up for not being good enough, or getting discouraged because what is being pointed out is something I have done again and again?

Day 8

VALUE HUMOR

Mark Twain once commented to someone who was solemn, unsmiling, and sanctimonious that it looked like he was waiting for a vacancy in the Trinity. Humor is very important in life—especially when it enables us to laugh at ourselves. Too often in our effort to take our important goals in life seriously, we take ourselves too seriously instead.

This is especially dangerous for those of us who deal with very sensitive issues and with people who are suffering. The nineteenth-century British writer Charles Kingsley was once speaking to a group of ministers who were so uptight that he couldn't loosen them up. Finally he quipped in frustration, "You know some ministers would make good martyrs. They are so dry, they would burn well."

Laughing at yourself can actually improve the work you do in difficult situations. Moreover, if you can't laugh at yourself, you run the real risk of burning out and not being able to continue the caring work you value so much. This is evident in parents who must care for children or for their aging parents or siblings. This is tough work, but it need not be devoid of humor.

A Simple Practice

Try to catch yourself when you are getting uptight and raining down condemnations on others who are not doing as much as they can. Step back. Remind yourself of Mark Twain's quote and tease yourself gently. It can make all the difference in difficult situations—especially chronic ones.

Day 9

———

REEVALUATE *your* COMPARISONS

A French proverb cautions: "What often makes us discontented with our condition is the absurdly exaggerated idea we have of the happiness of others."

I once had a patient who was discontent with his life although he had good health, a terrific wife and child, a thriving business, a house he owned outright, a fancy car, and rental properties. As I spent time with him I began to see that the reason he was so unhappy was that he would always make comparisons with others whom he saw as wealthier or seemingly happier.

We all have a tendency to compare ourselves with those we think have it better. We even buy magazines that feature such people, their houses, automobiles, boats, or other possessions.

It only dawns on us that such comparisons are foolish when we see others close up. Given my profession, I have worked with some who are famous, wealthy, and generally fall into the category of those whom the rest of us might be tempted to envy. The reality is they may have more stuff in their lives, but most of them spend a great deal of time protecting it rather than enjoying it. In contrast, many of us who are less important do have the time and freedom to enjoy what we have because we don't have to continually look over our shoulders to ensure no one is going to take it away.

Those who are worth emulating rather than envying are the people who have a spirit of serenity to enjoy all that they have been given and willingly share it freely with others without expecting anything in return. In this case, we seek to let their example inspire us, rather than be a comparison that deflates us. We can then incorporate into our lives good attitudes and activities such as taking a few moments each day to sit in silence, solitude, and gratitude; not worrying so much about our reputation; and appreciating what is, rather than what might be.

A Simple Practice

When you find yourself comparing yourself to others, take a step back so you can refocus yourself in a way that inspires rather than deflates. If you see someone who is good in many ways, let yourself be inspired to make little changes in your own behavior. If you see someone who has so much more than you, think about the many, many people who have not had a life as fortunate as yours. How we compare is the key to this practice. Remember that when it comes to contentment, the people who think money, good fortune, fame, and other such things represent real wealth often fail to be satisfied by their success. One of the themes of this book is: your ability to enjoy what is already available to you is an attitude of contentment. As a rabbi once said, "My gift is that I recognize I need something only after I already have it."

Day 10

SEE CHANGE *and* IMPROVEMENT *as an* ADVENTURE

Ask yourself: What *in me* blocks having a sense of clarity and contentment? Then plan a process of changing or modifying this style. Impossible to do? No. Just as habits are formed, they can be re-formed or balanced with a sense of patience, persistence, and curiosity about what helps or hinders your ability to see clearly, act correctly, and be content. With this approach even your failures are seen as teachers, and faithfulness to the process is valued as being more important than success.

One of the keystones of contentment is to recognize the need for openness to change and for willingness to overcome resistances to it. Resistance can be:

- Fear that change will take undue energy and disrupt your routine. (Yet, how much effort does it take to open your eyes and see? And, beyond this, why would you not want to breathe new energy into the stale air of your habits?)
- Concern that if you do change, others will react unfavorably. (The reality is that most people don't get up in the morning thinking of you, so your belief in their reaction is overstated. Plus, even if people do react,

they will soon get over it when they adjust to "the new you.")

- Worry that if you do begin to see new ways to live more freely—with greater space within yourself to offer others, to be someone who is open, generous, and loving to self and others— you will get disgusted with the fact that you have lived for so long without this joyous attitude in your life. (Yet readiness is a reality for us all; you probably weren't ready before, whereas now since you are reading this book and these words, you are.)

A Simple Practice

When you are contemplating new changes in your life, catch your temptations to ignore them or to feel that such new behaviors and attitudes are impossible. Tease yourself and become even more intrigued with how you might make friends with your resistances by seeing them as a natural part of yourself and the human condition. Come up with small steps toward what would be good and lifegiving for you and those who cross your path.

Day 11

SCHEDULE *and* HONOR "SABBATH TIME" *in* YOUR LIFE

Only in the past thirty years has psychology paid attention to solitude and silence. Classic spiritual wisdom writings have long been interested in it. What behavioral scientists found when they paid attention was that the capacity to be alone was tied to how healthy a person was and would remain.

My favorite story of the value of alone time is not from a psychologist or spiritual writer, though. It is from the Antarctic explorer Admiral Bird. When he went on a solo trip into this vast polar expanse, he wrote later about it in his diary. He noted that in addition to its scientific purpose, it was "one man's desire to know that kind of experience to the full, to be by himself for a while and to taste peace and quiet and solitude long enough to find out how good they really are. . . . I wanted to sink roots into some replenishing philosophy."

He then added, "I did take away something that I had not fully possessed before: appreciation of the sheer beauty and miracle of being alive, and a humble set of values. . . . Civilization has not altered my ideas. I live more simply now, and with more peace."

Clarity and contentment can be found anywhere—city, suburb, or countryside. Yet, wherever you live, you have a need to become silent for a while in a place of solitude. Doing this allows you to step back, breathe, and let unchecked compulsive thoughts and judgments rise to the surface to be seen before they settle to the bottom of your mental agenda. Fresh learning and living then become possible. Everyone, everywhere, needs to have and honor such Sabbath time in life.

A Simple Practice

Set some alone time during your day—even if it is only for a few moments—to sit quietly, breathe deeply, and break up the compulsive competition and routines that seem to strangle life. If possible, also take longer "Sabbath" times at home or in a place that offers you a chance for renewal.

Day 12

ENHANCE YOUR SENSE
of INNER EASE

When you have a sense of inner ease and are relaxed with yourself, you are not the only one who benefits; those around you do as well. You can experience this when you are with people who are not sarcastic, angry, arrogant, or overly competitive. When you are with people who seem to have a sense of stillness within themselves and offer a welcoming space, you feel the freedom being enhanced in yourself as well. By knowing and embracing your own gifts—and seeing them as just that: *gifts* not accomplishments—you are able to move among any group of people and feel at ease.

As I look back on those early years up on the farm, I remember happiness. Happiness of an ordinary, simple life. At times when I move away from the day's noise now, I am back there, or rather I find it reborn in me anew.

After a light summer rain, I take a walk and smell the fresh air, fields, and trees near my house, and I am home again, a child again, but this time not up on the farm but refreshed where I am.

On gray, cold winter days, I often remember the trip I took alone with my uncle Jack to visit the farm. It was not like the way I normally experienced the farm. The farm in winter was a desolate, seemingly lonely place. No summer visitors, no bustling efforts to bring the hay in before it rained. Just basic chores to be done, mist on the windows of a warm and well-lit kitchen, and a piece of pie and glass of milk alone with my aunt Anna.

I saw my uncle Mike's year-round helper, Johnny, slowly walking, hunched over because of an accident early in life, in a rhythm that wasn't the world's intense one.

No one present seemed disturbed on that winter visit. There was plenty of silence, and I felt it was powerful for me because I sensed no one had a desire to fill it with preoccupations, resentments, . . . with the *self*.

A Simple Practice

Take time to notice your ordinary, wonderful self. Don't look at how you or your situation can be improved. Instead, just smile and enjoy the reality of who you are—the very person that your friends and family enjoy and love. Simply being is not only a philosophical concept; more importantly, it is a way of living that is a gift to yourself and others around you.

Day 13

BE WARY *of* FALSE
EMOTIONAL HELPERS

Greed, anger, attachment, ignorance, fear, and inordinate self-centeredness often seem to come as our "helpers." After all, they remind us that we need, maybe even to our mind *deserve*, certain things in life. Yet these helpers are merely being sent by our ego to seduce us into having an unhelpful attitude toward life. We are living in an inner dictatorship.

When we live in a democracy we tend to take our inner freedom for granted while we are valuing being able to choose products, friends, or careers. Because we believe we are free, we rarely look at our habits, anxieties, and attachments. Yet an "inner democracy," which has nothing to do with the freedom to choose among different brands of soap, is what is often lacking. This produces anxiety and neediness.

A Simple Practice

When you are angry, fearful, resentful, or anxious about what you feel you need, deserve, or desire, ask yourself what thoughts are producing these negative feelings. Question these thoughts and feelings as to how they are imprisoning you within yourself, and they will lessen their hold and be shown for what they truly are—false helpers.

Day 14

PACE YOURSELF PROPERLY

In the fourth and fifth centuries, communities of monks developed in the Persian and North African deserts. The elders were called *ammas* (mothers) and *abbas* (fathers). They sought clarity, contentment, meaning, and inner peace. They often met with other searchers who wanted this as well. These searchers asked these wisdom figures for "a word"— some guidance on how they might find this spirit.

In response, they were given help, but always with an important proviso that is not very popular today: have patience. One desert father put it this way: "Don't try to understand everything; take on board what you can and make the most of it."

By doing this, those of us seeking the fresh streams of serenity (clarity, contentment, and compassion) will then not only avoid unnecessary discouragement, but also avoid the dangers of a tyranny of hope. Overestimating or underestimating what we or others can do can cause great problems.

A Small Practice

When you catch yourself being impatient with yourself, others, or situations, ask yourself: Did I do what I could?

What has this situation taught me? And what do I now believe would be a more reasonable pace for the progress and changes I wish would happen?

Day 15

DISCOVER *and* EMULATE
HEALTHY ROLE MODELS

Matthieu Ricard, in his wonderfully instructive book *Happiness*, notes that "meeting a few remarkable human beings who exemplify what a human life can be" can make all the difference in your life. Meeting such people now, in the past, or in books can be life-changing. Still, in finding a role model it is important to remember:

- We should seek to be inspired, encouraged, and challenged by such persons, not deflated or depressed by the fact that we don't presently live up to their model.
- The person we seek for us now might not be the same person who was a good role model for us in the past.
- We may not fully understand or like what such guides are teaching us.
- We need to be serious when we seek to take to heart their message.

A Simple Practice

Determine who in your present or past life is or was a healthy, wise role model for you. This can be done by reflecting on people in books as well as in your life who somehow have called you to be all that you can be without embarrassing you over where you are at this point. After doing that, list the attitudes or traits in these persons you wish to emulate. Try to put these goals into action. When you succeed, enjoy it and see what situations or people made the conditions favorable for good change. When you fail, be intrigued as to why this has happened and learn from that, too.

Day 16

KNOW *who* YOUR "GOD" REALLY *is*

We all have a center of gravity around which our energy flows. This is, by definition, our "god." As the saying goes, "Where your treasure is, your heart is too." It doesn't matter who or what we *say* is most important in our lives; it is our *behavior* that demonstrates what we really put first. Knowing where our energy is directed is very important, lest we delude ourselves into believing otherwise. The key is for us to seek the truth without psychologically attacking ourselves, because behavior that we wince at will eventually turn into behavior that we wink at. You can't continue to pick on yourself and expect to have the energy and interest for personal growth. It is better to look for the truth about what we value most (even if we don't initially like what we see) with a spirit of curiosity and hope. By being intrigued, patient, hopeful, and gentle with our explorations, much can be learned and accomplished.

A Simple Practice

Look at your thoughts, daydreams, reactions, and how you spend the time at your disposal. See what captures the biggest part of the time-pie. While doing this, review what goals you have and see how you view them. For instance, everyone wants their children to succeed. However, ultimately believing you can control this can cause a great deal of unnecessary tension. In this case, you have made a good into a god. Being aware of it, in the case of your children for example, can allow you to do what you can to help, but then to let go. The difference may sound minimal, but you will find it to be remarkable when you apply this approach to what preoccupies you.

Day 17

Nurture Compassionate Trust

When we are compassionate, we are not sending the message that people should trust us. Instead, we are communicating that we have trust in them. In doing this, we are sharing the attitude that we see gifts in them that they possibly believe were long lost. The offer is before them: what they had thought about themselves as being their best self can be experienced firsthand in this relationship.

A Simple Practice

When dealing with those who come to you for help—be they family, friends, coworkers, or new acquaintances—try to set the stage for the encounter by demonstrating trust in them. This is best done by avoiding arguing, belittling, or forcing them to believe what you do or to act as you wish. Instead, open up a space where they can rest their doubts, anger, resentment, stress, and anxieties and know you are (1) open to listening to them (2) willing to expend the energy on helping them gain as much clarity as possible and (3) willing to let them decide what path they wish to follow based on that new clarity.

Day 18

Nothing *is* Alien When
We *are* Mindful

When we are present to what is in our lives at the moment or when we are formally meditating, anything and everything that comes to mind is worthy. Annoyances, compulsions, disagreements, *everything*. Yet to allow these feelings, thoughts, understandings, and perceptions to be treated as worthy, we must see them nonjudgmentally and with a sense of intrigue—not with a sense of arrogance by projecting the blame on others, ignorance by blaming ourselves, or discouragement because we want them to go away. Everything is part of us; everything is worth examining and bringing home to integrate in our lives. When we do this, we will feel more energetic, free, and peaceful because the energy we had previously spent on resentment, shame, self-inflation, deflation, or defensiveness is now at our disposal to use for enjoying our lives and being helpful to others.

A Simple Practice

Greet reflections about yourself both clearly and gently. Image yourself as any mentor in your life who had eyes that were both kind and nonjudgmental. Be intrigued about what you don't like about yourself and embrace your negative thoughts as friends who can teach you new ideas and approaches with life. When you feel that you are seeing how exhibitionistic and ego-centered you are, don't deny it. Rather, remind yourself how much you have achieved given your good energy and ask why you felt the need to be so self-centered in a particular situation. When you find yourself condemning or gossiping about others, recognize how perceptive you are, but then ask why you might be tempted to use this skill against others. In other words, when you view your own "negative" behavior, remind yourself first about the gift behind this distortion of it and be intrigued about why and how the distortion arose in this specific situation.

Day 19

DEEPLY APPRECIATE
IMPERMANENCE

All major religions, philosophies, and psychologies remind us of a simple point that we usually ignore but which can help us live more attentively if we accept it: all births end in death and all gathering ends in losing. The Buddha put it well: "The trouble is you always think you have time."

Each day when you awake it is good to reflect on your fragility. You didn't die during the night. Today you might or might not die, but you have the day in front of you as far as you can see. The people you interact with—even those doing things you find annoying—are also in the same state as you: fragile. Knowing this, you might want to purify your motivations. You would want to be gentle and clear with others so you don't regret your last words or actions toward them.

This is the gift of deeply appreciating impermanence; it leads to a regular evaluation and correction of your motivations, actions, and reactions.

A Simple Practice

Check in with yourself in the morning to see if you realize, at a deep level, how fleeting life is and how impermanent everything is. Remind yourself:

- Everybody who is born, dies.
- Everything you have will eventually be lost.
- Everyone you now know will eventually leave you (through death or otherwise), or you will leave them.

A Buddhist image of the reality of impermanence and the fragility of life will help bring this to life. Life is like entering a boat that is going out onto the water to sink. This stark reality will wake you up to appreciate more deeply the brief time you and others have on this earth so you can be more attuned to honoring your own life and be truly compassionate to others (who are dying too).

Day 20

VALUE *Kenosis*

As I look back on the times I have spent in the country, I realize that they taught me that it was possible to live on less. They also taught me the paradox that living on less emptied me for so much more. And so I began to appreciate the free gifts of life and to appreciate the seasons—whether they be the seasons of the year or of a lifetime.

Just as my uncle's fields were allowed to lie fallow or were subject to crop rotation so the soil wouldn't be depleted of its nutrients, I needed to take similar steps. I needed to "lie fallow" at times by having periods alone, in quiet. These times might be as brief as ten minutes or half an hour in the morning, midday, or evening. They might be part of a weekend alone at home or a longer period up in the country. (Sometimes it is necessary to have longer periods to jumpstart the reflective habit again.)

Emptiness (known in the classic spiritual wisdom literature as *kenosis*) connects us with the inner seasons of our lives. We need to be able to listen to and respect the inner clock that allows us to be sensitive to each phase of our days, weeks, years, and lives. This comes when we have time to empty ourselves.

True *kenosis* is not a process of losing the good things in our lives. Instead, it is emptying ourselves so we can be fresh and open to receive what is next in our journey. To be content with each phase (season) of our lives, we have to be open to its gifts, challenges, and surprises. Some people seem stuck at a certain phase, be it their high school or college years, certain places of employment, or stages in family life. All of these may have been good times, and they don't need to be forgotten. Yet, unless they take a new place in our lives, they stifle us from breathing the fresh psychological and spiritual air of the *now* that is so necessary for contentment.

A Simple Practice

When the space within us is not cluttered by the past or preoccupied with the future, we experience *kenosis* and have both a clearer vision and a greater freedom. To encourage this, be inspired by the spiritual wisdom proverb: "If you relax with yourself, you can travel through any phase of your life and be among any group of people." A way to relax in this way is to simply sit and observe your breathing for a few moments. Breathing in, you feel the freshness of life; breathing out, you both let go of the past and exude love to all. If you feel that it is silly to observe and respect your breathing this way, just hold your breath and stop breathing for a while, and you will change your mind. People with severe asthma can certainly attest to the reality of knowing how precious breath is; you should honor it as well. Otherwise, you will end up with spiritual or psychological asthma and always be anxious, grasping, and in crisis, instead of breathing in an air of contentment and breathing out an air of compassion.

Day 21

Know How *to*
Measure Contentment
and Inner Freedom

Measuring your real inner freedom, which is a dear companion of contentment, is fairly straightforward. It includes such mental yardsticks as:

- How spontaneously negative emotions (anger, boredom, resentment, shame . . .) rise effortlessly to the surface.
- How often and easily you react with annoyance or anger during the day.
- How much time is spent daydreaming or obsessing about past losses, present desires, current frustrations, or future plans.

A Simple Practice

Watch for negative reactions you might have during the day, but greet them differently. Instead of anger, defensiveness, or excuses for having them, welcome them with a smile and ask them what they have to teach you about yourself. Keep greeting them this way, whether they lessen immediately or not, because faithfulness to the process, not immediate success, will bring greater contentment in your life. This is possible because you now see the negative reactions as teachers rather than simply as unpalatable moments to avoid at all cost.

Day 22

_____

CONSIDER *a* BIT LESS,
LIVE *a* BIT MORE

You are probably good at planning and preparation. If so, this is good. Good, that is, unless you center on that phase too much. It is like collecting menus all the time and either forgetting to order and eat the meal or only having a little time left in which to gobble it down.

When you stop grasping but have a simple sense of yourself and a clear sense of your purpose in life, your life becomes more existential, real, and present to you. When eventually death does arrive, it would be good for it to happen while you are truly living.

A Simple Practice

Simplify your life by choosing a word or name for yourself that reflects your central charism or gift. Ask your friends and family for help if it doesn't seem to be clear to you. (If need be, review the opening chapter.) Also, decide on a theme or philosophy for your life. (Mine is: *Be clear and be not afraid for you are loved by God.*) Use both the word and the philosophy for how you live out today. It will remind you to be present to yourself and others in ways that will help you live more and cut down on thinking about how you are living or should live in the future. Once you have defined your way of being present in the world, this way of being can effortlessly define the quality of each aspect of your life without your having to consider things too much.

Day 23

BEWARE *the* "FASTEST" ROUTE

A Russian proverb cautions, "You can't drive straight on a twisting lane." The same can be said about tacking a sloop; the quickest way to sail is not always what appears to be the straightest line to the opposite shore.

In the country, the paths I followed to get to the forest and back were never the straightest. On a very hot and humid day, as I left the forest for the fields I needed to cross, I wished I could just spirit myself straight up the hill, beyond which the shade of the barn and the house were waiting. However, I knew that if I tried a direct route (as I had a couple of times in the past), it would take me longer because of the climb and some pretty high barbed wire fences that kept the cows from roaming.

The same is the case in life. If we rush through life, we run the risk of missing helpful signs from nature or persons around us, or the promptings within that let us know what is best for us now.

A Simple Practice

During the day and when you are making a decision, stop yourself for a moment or two and check your feelings and thoughts. Explore them. This will help you to see how you might understand yourself a little better and what the interaction or event filling your mind is telling you. Good mentors have the gift of reflecting, not immediately reacting, when they are guiding people. We should emulate this when we are trying to be mentors to ourselves. Otherwise, we may move through life very quickly and efficiently, but in the wrong direction.

Day 24

A NEW DISCIPLINE,
a DIFFERENT DIRECTION

Shambhala is a Tibetan word for the inner spiritual journey. Persons who are good Buddhists dedicate themselves to this journey and seek good-heartedness within themselves and true compassion in how they live with others. This is "the land" they seek. Part of this process involves seeking to emulate, not merely admire, the example of other searchers who are more advanced, wise, and faithful.

Such seekers take small steps, virtuously giving true life to everything they do—small steps away from what is unhelpful and small steps toward developing wonderful habits. The journey progresses slowly, supported by an attitude of intrigue and a discipline of meditation or quiet time alone that is steady—no matter what may be going on in the world at the time.

A Simple Practice

When you are involved in important projects, take a moment to remind yourself that the most important project is *you*. With some quiet time established, especially when you are very busy, the quality of your life and your attitude toward your so-called "important" projects will improve immeasurably. Tell yourself this, and you will see how practical it is to take some time for yourself to nurture the inner life that is directing how and why you live the way you do.

Day 25

Practice What *you* Preach

You've heard this before, but it is truly a radical challenge for us to remember with a serious mind and open heart: *practice* what you preach. Contentment often spontaneously arises when our attitudes, actions, and words are all in line, when there is less incongruity and stress draining or distracting us from the essentials in life.

A Simple Practice

When you suggest something to someone or praise its value, remember the Spanish proverb and repeat it to yourself silently: "Tell me what you brag about and I'll tell you what you lack." After this, ask yourself two questions related to authenticity and true compassion: (1) How do these suggestions teach the values that I am sharing and claiming vibrantly in my life? (2) How practical are my suggestions to others given their abilities and what is already on their shoulders? (We want to be sure that we are doing something for people and not for our own, less than sensible and good, motivations.)

Day 26

KNOW WHAT "LIVING *in the*
MOMENT" REALLY MEANS

Appreciating the value of contentment involves recognizing
the time that can be wasted, either in regretting and resent-
ing the past or in being preoccupied with and daydreaming
about the future. As long as you are engaged in wasteful
patterns, you are missing the people and things that are in
your life now. "Living in the moment" sounds nice, but what
does it really mean?

At the very least, it means not postponing living until
you have everything perfectly in place or you feel you are
perfectly prepared. It means not wishing for another life or
framing your life in reverse by fixating on a time in the past
when you felt you were happy. When you do this, you are
dragging the past along in a way that leaves no energy for
life in the present.

A Simple Practice

When you find yourself in reverie about the past or future, complete the thought and then bring yourself back to
where you are. Listen to the person with you. Observe your
own reactions without judging them. Savor the coffee you

are drinking. Enjoy the food you have just placed in your mouth. Be aware of the smell of the ocean, the flow of traffic, the energy on the street, the calm in the field. Pay attention more and enjoy it!

Day 27

Enjoy Transparency

English country vet, James "Alf" Wight, who wrote under the pseudonym James Herriot, told wonderful stories about his life and work on the dales of northern England. Probably his most famous book was *All Creatures Great and Small*. One of the themes that came through in this book and the others he wrote was that being a country vet in those days was very difficult. The work was often grueling and the hours quite demanding.

In one of his stories he mentions that he had a particularly challenging case delivering a calf from a skinny little heifer stretched out on its side in an old shed that had little light and whose floor was strewn with bricks and junk. To make matters worse, he was working in tight quarters as the rain pelted his bare chest and arms through the open door while he sought to deliver a calf from the small heifer on this quiet inclement evening.

As he drove home, the reality of it all was hitting him because it was a Friday night and other people were already out enjoying themselves while he was driving in the dark, cold, miserable weather. As he entered one of the villages, he spotted the swinging sign of the Fox and Hounds, a small pub. He thought a beer and a visit to the warm pub would do him good, and he was confirmed in this feeling as he entered and noted a wood fire crackling in an old black cooking range.

He felt that he didn't need to share his misery but instead simply take in this bit of rest and renewal before driving all the way back home. As he approached the bar, Ted Dobson, the cowman who ran the place, said to him, "Now then, Mr. Herriot, you've been workin'." "Yes, Ted, how did you know?" The man glanced over Herriot's soiled mackintosh and the Wellington boots which he hadn't bothered to change after his evening on the farm and said, "Well, that's not your Sunday suit; there's blood on your nose end and cow shit on your ear." Then, Ted Dobson's face broke into a wide grin.

We often feel people don't know what we are going through, and sometimes this is true. However, people see more than we realize about our needs, defenses, desires, and ego trips, as well as our talents, kind actions, and gentle spirit.

Part of the reason our contentment is disturbed is because we spend so much energy trying to be different persons depending upon whom we are with. The best part about transparency and ordinariness is that we can always be the same person: genuine, integrated, open, and generous. The less we have to put on airs or seek to meet people's projections, the more we will feel genuine, transparent, *enough.*

A Simple Practice

Catch yourself when you are being someone other than yourself and tease yourself about it. Maybe you are speaking too much so as to get attention or impress people. Possibly it is the opposite, and you are hiding your helpful comments because of a fear of sharing your views. When you are defensive (opaque) the beauty of your ordinary self fails to shine, whereas when you are non-defensive (transparent) the games you play disappear. Then others are able to sense the psychological and spiritual space within you and in the process be encouraged to be themselves as well.

Day 28

KNOW *your* PERSPECTIVE . . .
then CHALLENGE IT!

A Buddhist canonical verse that Matthieu Ricard mentions in his book *Happiness* touches upon the power of perspective:

> For the lover, a beautiful woman is an object of desire,
> For the hermit, a distraction,
> For the wolf, a good meal.

How we perceive something or someone determines how we react. As a result, our perspective is a great tool for increasing or eliminating contentment in life.

The problem is that we assume that how we perceive something is totally true. It doesn't occur to us that we may be at least partially offbase, until a new event occurs or new information comes up that makes us realize how wrong we were.

Once when I was up on the farm, a family visited us. I noticed that the man paid a great deal of attention to a friend of mine. He was kind to me but particularly doted on my friend. As a result, it was a great surprise to me when my cousin told me that the man really was very impressed with me. In response, I said, "I didn't realize that. He seemed to pay so much attention to Jim." My cousin replied, "He did that because he knew Jim's father had died recently. But it was you he spoke about to me when we drove back to the city."

How often we make decisions about situations or people with little or even no information! In psychology we refer to this as "data-free analysis." We must remember that prejudice is not something that is created by full reason, and therefore it is not something that can be reasoned out of people—especially if they never question the veracity of it in the first place. The result is that we often predict negative things that disturb our sense of well-being, though they never happen. Similarly, we fail to see the positive things in life because we perceive that they are "no big deal" or miss them entirely. Therefore, enhancing our perspective is one of the most powerful things we can do if we wish to be content in and with life.

A Simple Practice

Sense when you have strong feelings about a person, event, or issue, and then be a devil's advocate and challenge your own views. It will not only help you broaden your understanding of yourself and what and how you are judging someone or something, it will also demonstrate how powerful uncovering and altering one's perceptions can be—for the good.

KNOW YOUR COPING STYLE *and* YOU WILL DISCOVER *your* ACHILLES' HEEL

If you are aware of your basic coping style and what you are trying to accomplish when you are under stress, you will find it possible to recognize the desires and problems that might result. In this way, you can continue to use your style but recognize that, as in the case of all styles, it has limits. Knowing this is very helpful because when cautions arise they can be picked up rather than ignored or denied.

To be aware of our coping style is necessary if we wish to be content. Otherwise, our sense of inner ease will be disrupted by feelings that we are being let down or paying too much for our style in life. We will fail to see our style as good, although one that needs to be pruned occasionally through the use of other approaches. For example:

- If you seek to be perfect in what you do, then you run the risk of always chasing approval. The problem in this is that, while it is great to have high goals, instead being inspired, we feel condemned by them, focus too much on details, and often become irritated with others' efforts and supposed expectations of us.

- If you seek to be nice to others, the risk is that you are, in turn, expecting the reward that they will be nice to you and show you appreciation. When this doesn't happen, resentment may soon follow. And you may fail to see that it is faithfulness, not success or personal reward, that is important.
- If you seek to work hard and constantly, you risk being exhausted, always on the run, and unhappy with the process. You also risk feeling you never complete all the tasks you set out to do. You will feel restless on the one hand, but on the other you will feel you really should have more time for leisure.
- Finally, you may seek to be tough when confronted with difficulties. While this is a good coping skill, you run the risk of becoming "the lone stranger" because people will feel you don't need or want their help. As a result, you will feel no one cares, or you will become so distant from your feelings that you will be callous and lose the joy of experiencing both the ups and downs of life.

One summer morning when I awoke on the farm and came down to breakfast, the atmosphere seemed a bit down. When I asked what was the matter, they said that Poochie, my uncle Mike's dog, had been chasing a truck and had been hit. He was dragged for one hundred yards and had been killed. The driver was so upset that he came to my uncle and told him what had happened. My uncle told the driver it wasn't his fault. Poochie's gift was that he loved to chase and corral the cows, but his problem was that he also liked to chase trucks and was almost hit hundreds of times. This time he didn't make it.

Like Poochie, we have gifts and growing edges that are tied together. We can't get rid of our problem areas; they are connected to our gifts. However, we would benefit immensely by recognizing when our gifts become problematic and then pruning them. We can take a step back, see what is distorting our talents, and address the situation before we hurt ourselves or others by being pulled into a situation that can cause real harm.

A Simple Practice

Know your gifts. Make a list of them and don't be bashful. These, in the language of positive psychology, are our signature strengths. We have been gifted with them at birth. They were enhanced in the early years of our life, and if we have been wise, we have been nurturing them ever since because they make us helpful, attractive, and constructive. Now, after that, make another list of things you and others find annoying, defensive, and destructive about you and see how they are connected to the very gifts you have. Following this, seek each day to see when and how your gifts become problematic for you and others. For instance, if you are energetic and passionate, when do you become intrusive and controlling? If you are bright and analytic, when do you become so heady that you miss the feelings and personal issues involved in an interaction? The information gained will not result in eliminating your basic style of interaction. Instead, it will enhance it, just as in pruning a bush you increase its blossoms. Moreover, such an awareness of yourself results in avoiding and lessening the discontent such personality downsides may cause for you and others.

Day 30

———

IMPROVE YOUR SENSE *of* MINDFULNESS

Mindfulness is being in the present moment with your eyes open to what is truly before you. While this sounds simple—and as a principle it is—it is not easy. But there are questions you can ask yourself that on the one hand lessen mindlessness and on the other increase mindfulness. Such questions will help you make mindfulness real in your life and help raise your awareness of how you are on automatic pilot much of the time. The more mindful you are able to be, the more content you will be that the life you are living is as real and full as it can be. Mindfulness is *that* important.

In a book I wrote recently that had a section on mindfulness (*Bounce: Living the Resilient Life*), I included an admonishment by Jon Kabat-Zinn that powerfully communicates this; I would like to include it here as well on this last day of your retreat:

> If what happens now does influence what happens next, then doesn't it make sense to look around a bit from time to time so that you are more in touch with what is happening now, so that you can take

your inner and outer bearings and perceive with clarity the path that you are actually on and the direction in which you are going? If you do so, maybe you will be in a better position to chart a course for yourself that is truer to your inner be-ing—a soul path, a path with heart, your path with a capital P. If not, the sheer momentum of your unconsciousness in this moment just colors the next moment. The days, months, and years quickly go by unnoticed, unused, unappreciated.

It is all too easy to remain on something of a fog-enshrouded, slippery slope right into our graves; or, in the fog-dispelling clarity which on occasion precedes the moment of death, to wake up and realize that what we had thought all those years about how life was to be lived and what was important were at best unexamined half-truths based on fear or ignorance, only our own life-lim-iting ideas, and not the truth or the way our life had to be at all.

No one else can do this job of waking up for us, although our family and friends do sometimes try desperately to get through to us, to help us see more clearly or break out of our own blindness. But waking up is ultimately something that each of us can only do for ourselves. When it comes down to it, wherever *you* go, there *you* are. It's *your* life that is unfolding.

A Simple Practice

To break the habit of mind*less*ness, the following small steps can produce surprisingly big results:

- At several intervals during the day, sit back for a few moments, observe your breath, counting each exhale from one to four and repeating this process as you feel your body relax.
- Smile when you can during the day; frowns and negative thoughts often arise spontaneously out of habit. This will break this cycle and allow you to be more mindful and grateful.
- Image a serene, contented friend and take out time to "just be" while picturing yourself as that person.
- Give yourself opportunities to flow by not wasting energy by avoiding, arguing, or resisting aspects of your life. Instead, welcome them home. When that happens, what was boring, distracting, or unpleasant can be quietly transformed by reflection and an openness to see everything as a teacher.
- Use cues (telephone rings, a smile from a colleague, computer beeps, a baby crying) to remind yourself to relax and be present.
- Eat more slowly, taste your food, and enjoy the coolness or warmth of what you are drinking.
- Enjoy (rather than complain about) surprising, potentially mindful periods such as standing in line, being caught in traffic, or waking in the middle of the night.
- Catch yourself when you are harsh with yourself or others, and see it as an opportunity to learn to be more patient.

- Remember the fun you had with "the little things" in life, and seek to enjoy opportunities to be childlike in your approach to life now.

(For other suggestions, I have included recommended readings as well as further information on mindfulness in my books *Prayerfulness: Awakening to the Fullness of Life* and *Bounce: Living the Resilient Life*. I have found this area personally and professionally very rewarding and look for opportunities whenever I can to share material on it with others.)

A QUESTION *of* CONTENTMENT: REFLECTING, NOT REACTING

When I lived on the farm during the summer, part of the fun was being able to invite friends. They always enjoyed themselves, and I loved the company. When I did receive such visitors, hunting was usually on our agenda, although I could never get into it. Fishing was more of an interest to me. Just being outdoors by a stream, deep brook, or lake was enough for me. I was happy if I caught a trout or pickerel, but I didn't count on it; I usually wasn't smarter than the fish.

Once, a visiting friend decided he was going to go hunting, and I decided to go fishing instead. We planned to catch up later in the day and swap our experiences. All of the adults would be away for the full day doing other things.

Just before noon I decided to return home. It was getting too hot to catch anything, and I had gotten a few nibbles on the line but nothing much else.

I was surprised to find my friend at home when I returned. He usually stayed out until mid-afternoon no matter how hot it got. He was relaxing on the lawn, drinking a Coke and swatting away the occasional fly.

I told him I had fun, but had terrible luck at the lake, and asked how he had made out. He said he had thought it was going to be great. Early on he had seen some woodchucks that were digging holes in the field where my uncle planted crops. They were a real nuisance. If you weren't careful, a horse or even a person could break a leg by unexpectedly stepping into one of their holes.

However, he said he missed a few shots and decided to return to the house. There were some rodent pests driving us nuts that he thought he might see—especially since no one was at home—but a small plane kept buzzing the house so he didn't have a chance of that happening.

I responded that it often happens, and there is little you could do about it. He said, "Oh, no, I did something about it. I waved him off."

I laughed and said, "I'll bet that did a lot of good!"

"You're right," he said. "He just kept coming, so I went into the house and got my shotgun out and shook it at him."

"I'm sure he didn't pay attention to that. He knew you would never shoot at him."

"You're right. He didn't pay attention at all. He was flying so slow I could see him laugh at me."

"So, what did you do next? Did you just go inside and have a Coke? That's what I would do. He would finally get tired of it and go away."

"No. I aimed the shotgun at him."

I made a face and said, "He knew you weren't going to shoot."

"Well, he knew wrong. I did."

"You *what?*"

"I shot at him."

"Are you crazy? It's lucky you didn't hit him."

"Actually, I did. You could hear the pellets hit one of the wings."

"What!"

"Well, he didn't fly over the house again."

Sometimes the reactions we have as teenagers and even later as adults can be truly amazing. The fact that more of them don't end in disaster is pure grace.

However, even though we may mature in many ways, one tendency that doesn't disappear and may even increase is the opposite problem: getting caught in a rut and failing to react in creative new ways. The result for us as adults "who should know better" is to be trapped by our own habits, style of thinking, and perceptions.

Instead of being mindful of the wonderful experiences present in the now, we fall into nostalgia or preoccupation about the future. In place of gratefulness and contentment, we look out the window and wish for something or someone else in our lives and take no constructive steps to move ahead. We fall prey to little negative quips such as, "These are not the golden years. These are the rusty years."

This book stands against that philosophy. It asks that we step back and reflect rather than react. Then our thoughts can be clear, our beliefs filled with gratitude. Then we can *act*—not with malice or ego-centeredness—but with joy and compassion.

This may seem like a tall order for a short book, but the attitude underlying it is that the process of exploring contentment will bring rewards for you and those you encounter.

Contentment cannot be sought directly. To do so would result in selfish, hedonistic behavior and would not achieve the goal anyway. Instead, this book has tried to open up consideration of new streams of contentment. These streams include grateful eyes, mindfulness, a compassionate heart that expects nothing from those we help, and an appreciation of simplicity so our ego doesn't cause us unnecessary anxiety, discouragement, and stress.

Now that you have read this book, I would like to suggest that you take a few additional moments with each of the questions listed below. They are designed to call you to delve more deeply into your own attitudes, perceptions, and ways of being.

My hope is that they will also help you discover your own ways to live with a little more clarity, simplicity, compassion . . . and *contentment*. This is not just about you; when you have space within yourself to enjoy what is truly essential for contentment, you are in a position to offer this space to others as well. And what greater gift could you give to others in such stressful, confusing times? As I often emphasize in my presentations and writings, one of the greatest things you can share with others is a sense of your own peace and healthy perspective, but you can't share what you don't have. It is as simple and challenging as that and a worthy reason to reflect on the following questions.

Twenty Questions on the Streams of Contentment

1. What is your central talent, gift, or charism? How are you feeding and pruning it so it can be enjoyed by both you and others?

2. What is critical to your own well-being in the long run (friendship, quiet time, continual learning, healthy, fun activities . . .) and how are you ensuring these elements are in place in your life?

3. What is your attitude toward reaching out to others? Can you get more excited about being faithful to the process of caring rather than be caught up in the need for success or appreciation?

4. How are you able to let go of preoccupations with past events or future fantasies so you can be more present to the grandeur of your present life as it unfolds?

5. Are you letting the fragility of life wake you up so you don't fall into the trap of thinking you will always have time?

6. Can you seek to let past hurts soften your soul rather than embitter you? If so, given your personality, how is it best done?

7. Do you check in with your friends in person, over the phone, or via e-mail, or do you say you are too busy now and put them off?

8. When you interact with family, friends, and coworkers, are you able to have low expectations and high hopes so you don't try to force them to do or be what you want and thus avoid anger on their part and frustration on yours?

9. When tough times come (and they do for everyone), are you able to lean back in the darkness and see what you can learn rather than simply to react against it?

10. Can you embrace the paradox of gratefulness each day, so you can realize the truth that to those who are appreciative more will be given?

11. Are you able to take at least five minutes each day in silence, solitude, wrapped in gratitude so you can center yourself as you face the next moments of your life?

12. Are you able to break up your busy day by taking a few breaths, smiling, and saying, "What I have is enough. I am enough."

13. Are you able to take a step back when you fail, make a mistake, or are criticized and seek to be intrigued by your feelings, thoughts, and what you can learn, rather than merely being defensive to others, offensive to yourself, or discouraged that you are not a better person?

14. Can you tease yourself a bit more when you are making a big deal out of things?

15. Are you able to whisper to yourself at the beginning and end of each day, "Life is a gift. I am a gift. Thank you. Thank you."

16. How can you live more and plan less?

17. How can you call yourself back to the present when you are distracted?

18. What unfinished business, habits, past pains, or pleasurable moments are you holding onto or attached to that prevent you from really experiencing your life with a sense of simplicity, clarity, and contentment *in the present moment*?

19. Who are the most content people you know, and what steps would you like to take to be like them *now*?

20. What do you need to trade in your current style of dealing with the world for the joy of inner freedom?

Works Cited

Bausch, William. *A World of Stories for Preachers and Teachers.*
Byrd, Richard. *Alone.*
Covey, Stephen. *The 7 Habits of Highly Effective People.*
de Mello, Anthony. *One Minute Wisdom.*
Epstein, Mark. *Psychotherapy without the Self.*
Fulghum, Robert. *All I Really Need to Know I Learned in Kindergarten.*
Georgiou, S.T. *The Way of the Dreamcatcher.*
Herriot, James. *All Creatures Great and Small.*
Hoff, Benjamin. *The Te of Piglet.*
Johnson, Sandy. *The Book of Tibetan Elders.*
Kabat-Zinn, Jon. *Wherever You Go, There You Are.*
May, Gerald. *The Dark Night of the Soul.*
Montaigne, Michel de. *Selected Essays.*
Mott, Michael. *The Seven Mountains of Thomas Merton.*
Norris, Kathleen. *Dakota.*
Nouwen, Henri. *The Genesee Diary.*
Ricard, Matthieu. *Happiness.*
Sotile, Wayne, and Mary Sotile. *The Resilient Physician.*
Stokes, Gillian. *Contentment.*
Storr, Anthony. *Solitude.*
Strand, Clark. *The Wooden Bowl.*
Wicks, Robert. *Crossing the Desert.*
Zafón, Carlos Ruiz. *The Shadow of the Wind.*

Recommended Reading

A short list of books I have found encouraging on how to live with greater simplicity, compassion, and contentment

Bode, Richard. *First You Have to Row a Little Boat.*
Braza, Jerry. *Moment by Moment.*
Chadwick, David. *Crooked Cucumber.*
Chodron, Pema. *When Things Fall Apart.*
Crane, George. *Bones of the Master.*
de Mello, Anthony. *One Minute Wisdom.*
Dillard, Annie. *The Writing Life.*
France, Peter. *Hermits: The Insights of Solitude.*
Frankl, Viktor. *Man's Search for Meaning.*
Georgiou, S.T. *The Way of the Dreamcatcher.*
Harvey, Andrew. *A Journey in Ladakh.*
Irvine, William. *On Desire.*
Johnson, Sandy. *The Book of Tibetan Elders.*
Merton, Thomas. *The Wisdom of the Desert.*
Norris, Kathleen. *Dakota.*
Nouwen, Henri. *The Genesee Diary.*
Nouwen, Henri. *Making All Things New.*
Ricard, Matthieu. *Happiness.*
Rilke, Rainer Maria. *Letters to a Young Poet.*
Rinpoche, Sogyal. *The Tibetan Book of Living and Dying.*
Simmons, Philip. *Learning to Fall: The Blessings of the Imperfect Life.*
Storr, Anthony. *Solitude.*
Strand, Clark. *The Wooden Bowl.*

ACKNOWLEDGMENTS

Spiritual poet Rumi remarked on the power of story. Stories get into your heart and change it in ways other lessons could not. I have found that this is no exaggeration, so I am deeply grateful that the following people have shared stories, quotations, and reflections with me to include in this book: Luise Ahrens, Carol Barry, Mel Blanchette, Joe Ciarrocchi, Brendan Geary, William Guri, Carole O'Keefe, Karen Schneider, Jim Storms, Dennis Tindall, and Ray Wicks.

The Sorin Books team (Tom Grady, Bob Hamma, Karey Circosta, Julie Cinninger, and Amanda Williams) as usual were great to work with because they seamlessly combine the professional and the personal in such beautiful, meaningful ways. I'm grateful.

Mary Catherine Bunting has been a faithful supporter of my work on the prevention of secondary stress—especially of my travels to work with professionals in the healing and helping professions from around the world. I shall always be deeply appreciative. Her encouragement was there at just the times I needed it.

Another person who believed in my work in helping people under stress to regain a healthier sense of perspective is Judith Needham. Her graciousness in going out of her way to introduce me and my work to new audiences demonstrates a generativity and trust in me that I find wonderfully supportive. It also challenges me to see how I can be of even greater service to others. Thank you, Judith.

Finally, the person to whom I give a short manuscript and she returns it to me even shorter, my personal editor, lover, best friend, and wife, Michaele Barry Wicks. I thank you for your patience, love, wisdom, and understanding.

***

Stories in this book are composites so as to protect the privacy of individuals. As a result, no one person cited is real, but the themes presented are true.